ENGLISH PROVINCIAL POSTS
1633-1840

The Dover mail coach passes a stage coach at a wayside inn. Thought
to have been painted and engraved by R. Havell. (By courtesy of the
Post Office)

English Provincial Posts

1633-1840

A study based on Kent examples

by

BRIAN AUSTEN

PHILLIMORE

1978

Published by
PHILLIMORE & CO. LTD.,
London and Chichester

Head Office: Shopwyke Hall,
Chichester, Sussex, England

ISBN 0 85033 266 4

Printed in Great Britain by
UNWIN BROTHERS LTD.,
at The Gresham Press, Old Woking, Surrey
and bound by
THE NEWDIGATE PRESS LTD.,
at Book House, Dorking, Surrey

CONTENTS

PREFACE

SINCE the late 19th century the development of the British Post Office and the conveyance of mails has interested both professional historians and dabblers in anecdote and romance with predictable results. Sound general histories, based mainly on printed primary sources such as Howard Robinson's *The British Post Office—a History* (Princeton 1948), provide a valuable outline. More detailed studies of particular aspects are rare, though a notable exception is Kenneth Ellis, *The British Post Office in the Eighteenth Century* (1958). In striking contrast to such scholarly approaches is the considerable volume of nostalgic coaching literature produced in the last two decades of the 19th century—the reminiscences of those who saw the death of long distance coaching while they were in their youth. Later writers in the field have mainly used this quarry of anecdote to feed the legend of the romance of the mail coaching days.

A study of the method by which the Post Office administered its operations outside London is needed to fill out the picture, and this to date has been lacking. It is hoped that this book will help to fill this gap. The area chosen to exemplify provincial postal administration is the county of Kent which provides a unique opportunity for such a study. No other county contains the complete length of a main post road from London, and the post road is a more viable unit of study than the county. Kent has within its boundaries not only the Dover Road, so vital for communication with the continent, but also most of the post road to Rye and Hastings. A study of the postal history of Kent illustrates well the rise of both inland and seaside spas, military activity during the Napoleonic Wars and the development of local postal traffic in the form of fifth clause and penny posts. Excluded from the study, however, are the areas, once part of the county, near to the metropolis such as Woolwich, Erith, Greenwich, Lewisham, New Cross and Blackheath served by the London District Post.

Although this book is aimed mainly at the economic and social historian with an interest in the history of transport and communications, and the local historian interested in Kent, it may also assist the growing number of persons who find relaxation in the study of the postal history and postal markings of their locality. This group will immediately regret the absence of check lists of handstamps but it is hoped that their gain will be to see the pattern of local postal administration in perspective.

This study would not have been possible without the support provided by a large number of institutions and individuals. A special word of thanks must be given to the staff of the Post Office Record Office who have patiently provided documents from their archives, answered countless enquiries and provided valuable assistance throughout. They have borne the brunt of my research, but I have found an equal desire to assist wherever I have sought information, and I am sincerely indebted to The British Library, The Customs and Excise Record Office, The East Sussex Record Office, The Guildhall Library, The House of Lords Record Office, The Kent Archives Office, The National Maritime Museum, The Public Record Office, Harringey Public Libraries (Bruce Castle, Tottenham Collection) and the Library of the University of Kent.

The text has been greatly enhanced by the valuable assistance and encouragement provided by Professor T. C. Barker of the University of Kent who over a period of several years took an interest in the project. I am also thankful for encouragement to publish and for suggestions regarding the final form of the text to Professor W. H. Challoner of the University of Manchester and Professor A. M. Everitt of the University of Leicester. My final thanks are due to my colleague Peter Checkley who read the text and made a number of suggestions which have removed obscurities and improved the general presentation.

BRIAN AUSTEN

Chapter 1

THE KENTISH POSTS UNDER CHARLES I AND THE COMMONWEALTH, 1633-60

THE NEED for the king to communicate by letter with other rulers is as old as diplomacy itself, and the need for merchants to communicate by letter is as old as trade. In Britain, before the 16th century, posts were set up by the king as needs directed and were not of a permanent nature. Merchants employed their own servants, other travellers, or carriers to convey their letters.

The greater involvement in European affairs during the reign of Henry VIII, and the increased administrative burden at home resulting from the greater centralisation of government, led to the appointment of Sir Brian Tuke as the first Master of the Post. The only regular post route maintained, however, was that from London to Calais by way of Dover. In theory, postal routes were established to Berwick and Edinburgh in the north, to Ireland by way of Holyhead, and to Falmouth in the west, but these were intermittently maintained and only used regularly in times of stress.

Despite the irregularity of the royal postal service in the 16th and early 17th centuries attempts were made to force people exclusively to use it. The Reformation had created a situation in which the bitter strife between catholic and protestant threatened the peace of Europe. In England frequent catholic plots to depose Elizabeth I and restore the old faith made vigilence essential.

By having a monopoly of the carriage, especially of foreign letters, the government could note who was corresponding with others overseas and open the letters of those suspected of plotting against the State. For reasons of security it was also necessary to know who was travelling, and the government was anxious through a system of postmasters to establish a monopoly of the hire of horses for through journeys. A royal

1

monopoly of all mail to and from foreign parts was proclaimed
by Queen Elizabeth I in 1591, and this was reinforced in 1603
by a further proclamation reserving the right to hire horses for
travel to the postmasters who horsed the royal posts. Both
measures were only partially effective.

In order to improve the efficiency of the service Mathew de
Quester, a native of Bruges, was appointed Postmaster for
Foreign Parts in 1619. Although under his care routes were
maintained to France, Flanders and the Netherlands for both
state and private correspondence, the service left much to be
desired. Dissatisfaction led the Merchant Adventurers in 1627
to appoint their own post master, which brought a sharp rebuke
from Sir John Coke, Charles I's Principal Secretary of State.
To allay criticism de Quester was dismissed in 1632, and Thomas
Witherings and William Frizell were appointed in his place.
Thomas Witherings, a London merchant and holder of the
appointment of Harbinger to the Queen was the dominant
partner. He denounced the slackness of de Quester's service
claiming that it was taking 14 days for a letter to reach London
from Antwerp and 15 hours was needed to carry mails from
Dover to the capital.[1] He accused de Quester's agents of:

> minding their own peddling traffic more than the service of the
> State or merchants, omitting many passages, sometimes staying
> for the vending of their own commodities, many times through
> neglect by lying in tippling houses.

A plan was presented to Sir John Coke by Thomas Witherings
to bring order to the posts. He claimed that the speed of his
service would render the sending of express letters by special
courier on State matters unnecessary. This alone would save the
King £1,000 to £1,500 each year. Posts were to be organised on
the best continental pattern, with postboys riding from stage to
stage day and night until the letter bags were delivered. Mails
in the past had been entrusted to common carriers and even
foreigners. Coke agreed to Withering's plan to set up these
'Staffeto' or express posts, and he was appointed Foreign Postmaster in place of de Quester. He was required to establish an
office in London for the receipt and distribution of letters.[2]

Mails were to be despatched at regular times, and a notice
was placed in the door of the Foreign Postmaster's office
informing people to bring their letters

for way of Antwerp everie friday, for way of France everie wednesday & for that of Holland everie Saterday al to be in the office
before five in the afternoone.

A register was to kept of all the letters posted indicating both
sender and addressee. Letters were to be sealed in a bag and
despatched by 6 pm, in order to reach Dover early the next
day 'that ther may be sufficient day light for passage over sea
the same day' Agreements were made with postmasters on the
Dover Road to see that they had

sufficient horses and messingers alwaies in redinesse, to go forth
with the pacquets with out aine delay and to deliver them from
stage to stage within the compasse of an hour & half for enene
stage.

A label was to be attached to the mail bag on which postmasters were to record the day and hour received to check
any slackness. By these means it was hoped to reduce the time
in transit between London and Antwerp from eight days or
more to no longer than three days.

Packet boats at Dover were ordered to sail 'the same hower
the pacquet cummeth if extremitie of weather hinder not',
and were not to linger for any further passengers and cargo.
The messenger carrying the mails sailed with the packet and
was to obtain a receipt from the mails from the Calais postmaster in order that the Foreign Postmaster in London could
produce it, if required, as evidence of delivery. If the weather
was adverse and the boat had to make for an alternative continental port the messenger was to hire a horse and deliver the
mails to the nearest post office on its destined route. Witherings
was instructed to negotiate with the postmasters of Calais,
Antwerp and Paris for the onward conveyance of the mails.[3]

On 8 April 1633 Thomas Witherings was at Calais, and in a
letter addressed to 'Right Honerable and my good patron',
Sir John Coke, he reported his progress.[4] Talks had been conducted with the Postmaster of Ghent and the Secretary to the
Countess Taxis. The Counts of Taxis were heriditary postmasters
of the Holy Roman Empire, and as such were responsible for
an extensive system of postal routes in Central Europe and the
north and east of France. Witherings was able to report that in
seven days time the new London to Antwerp staffeto post
would commence. He found difficulty, however, in locating a

boatman prepared to give the mails priority over passengers and goods.

> The boatmen of this place who take their turns for Dover I find unwilling to be obliged to depart upon the coming of the Portmantell.

With the help of English merchants he did, however, find a boatman willing to undertake the work on his terms.

> I have found out a very sufficient man who will oblige himself with security that for 40 shillings he will wait upon the coming of the packet, upon sight whereof he will depart, engaging himself to carry nothing but the said packet.

Witherings indicated that he would stay and see the first mail through from Antwerp by this new method of conveyance.[5]

Negotiations with the French post office for further continental routes were conducted by Philip Burlamachi, a naturalised foreigner who had become an important London merchant, the agent of Charles I in raising loans in the City, and in 1640 was to take over the Foreign Post from Witherings. On 7 December 1633 Burlamachi wrote to Sir John Coke detailing arrangements made by the Paris postmaster for a faster service between London and Paris.

> On pourra avoir lettres de Paris ici en 5 jours et moins, et ainsi les faire tenir la, ou de present ills demeurent 14 hours a venir.[6]

A postal treaty was signed with M. Denoveau, the French postmaster, and ratified on 13 April 1637, to come into force on 11 February the following year.[7] This enabled mails bagged in London for Boulogne, Abbeville or Amiens to be prepared, and the Dover to Calais route was declared to be the only permitted cross-channel service. Letters were forbidden to pass between Rye and Dieppe, and the Mayors of Rye, Dover, and Canterbury were instructed to assist Witherings maintain this monopoly. With all letters forced into one entry point a greater surveillance of overseas correspondence was possible.

Witherings' efforts probably did not meet with the success that he so confidently forecast. An undated petition included in the 1635-6 volume of the *Calendar of State Papers Domestic*[8] mentions complaints of delay. Some of the points of the 1633 regulations are repeated, as if not yet in force. The petition is in the names of Thomas Witherings and his partner, William

Frizell, 'his Ma^ts. Postmasters for foaringne parts' and addressed
to Sir John Coke. The petitioners asked for a set hour of departure from London, so that the mail could sail from Dover early
next day, and the setting up of stages every 10 or 12 miles from
Dartford, each to keep two good horses and a messenger ready,
both points listed in the 1633 regulations. Mention is made of
the settlement of routes to Germany, Italy and Flanders by the
Antwerp postmaster for the English mails, and the petitioners
stated their scheme would allow mail to reach London from
Antwerp in two and a half days in summer, and three and a
half in winter.

Thomas Witherings' attention was also directed to the inland
posts which he took over in 1635. At this time the posts were
costing Charles I £3,400 per year to operate, despite the poor
service provided. Witherings' plan was to convert all the existing
inland posts to the staffeto pattern which he had already put
into operation on the Dover Road. Times of departure were
to be regular, and to help cover the cost, the public were to
be encouraged to use the service. A letter consisting of one
sheet of paper (a single letter) was to be carried up to 80 miles
for 2d., 80 to 100 miles for 4d., and beyond that 8d. to the
borders of Scotland.

Withering's plan[9] was submitted on 14 June to Sir John
Coke. Routes were to be maintained to Scotland, Ireland,
Bristol, Shrewsbury, Plymouth, Dover, Harwich, and Yarmouth.
The existing footposts which had been able to travel 16 to
18 miles a day were to be replaced by riders travelling day and
night and covering 120 miles. The posts would provide a valuable intelligence network especially from the south coast, where
information obtained from shipping or travellers could
speedily be transmitted to London. Witherings declared that

> Anie fight at Sea; any distress of his Ma^ts shipps (which God forbid)
> anie wrong offered by anie other nation to any of the Coastes of
> England, or anie of his Ma^ts forts; the Post being punctually paid,
> the news will come sooner than thought.[10]

The ideas were accepted, and on 31 July of the same year a
Royal Proclamation was issued setting up 'the Letter Office
of England and Scotland'.[11] Witherings was named as the agent
by which the plan was to be put into effect. Improved speeds
were to take a letter to Edinburgh and back in six days

compared with two months by the previous foot posts. Rates
were for the first time laid down for inland letters. These were
2d. for a single letter under 80 miles, 4d. for 80 to 140 miles,
6d. for distances in excess of 140 miles, and 8d. to Scotland.
Monopoly rights were given to Witherings and mayors and local
officials were directed to support him in the execution of his
plans. Postmasters were to receive 2½d. per mile for horse hire
and were to maintain either one or two horses as directed,
and these were not to be hired out on the days the post was
due.

A Grant of Patent under the Privy Seal dated 22 June 1637
appointed Witherings postmaster for life and expanded the
regulations of 1635.[12] The maximum stay at any one stage was
limited to a 'half a quarter of an hower at the most', and speeds
of transit were laid down as seven miles an hour in summer, and
five in winter. Details of four post roads were given, including
the Dover Road on which seven stages were listed at Dartford,
Gravesend, Rochester, Sittingbourne, Canterbury, and Dover.
Deal was also listed. All postmasters on this road were to .
receive a salary of a shilling a day for their services, except for
the Gravesend postmaster, who was to receive sixpence. The
Dover Road thus accounted for a daily expense for salaries of
7s. 6d. out of a total salary account nationally for all roads of
£5 12s. 10d.

Witherings' plans for improving the service were no doubt
optimistic, failing to take fully into account the tools with
which they would have to be put into effect. Postmasters
nationally had one strong grievance. Their salaries were badly in
arrears, and no doubt their co-operation with their employers
was in consequence far from complete. A petition of all the
postmasters in England presented in 1628 claimed that they had
received no payment for seven years and were owed £22,000.
Two years later it had risen to £25,535, and by 1637 to
£60,000.[13] A petition from the Sandwich postmaster believed
to date from 1635 mentions arrears of £255 10s. 0d., covering
the last 10½ years years, while the Dartford postmaster was
owed £100, representing two and a half years arrears. He claimed
that as a consequence of not being paid he dared 'not go abroad
for fear of arrest by creditors by whom he has been furnished
with hay and other provisions.' Some payments did

materialise eventually, and on 27 July 1637 warrants for pay-
ment were issued for a number of postmasters, including James
Ware of Dartford, Thomas Lord of Gravesend, and Richard
Jennings of Sittingbourne.[14]

One of the main duties of the postmasters was to see that the
messenger carrying the regular mail, or letters sent express, was
provided with a fresh and sufficient mount for the journey to
the next stage. They also enjoyed a monopoly of providing
post horses for travellers, and thus kept many more horses than
those required to undertake the postal duty. The Dartford
postmaster petitioning for arrears of pay in 1635 declared that
he was 'forced to keep sixteen horses for the performance of
the service which is an extremely great charge'. Providing post
horses to travellers must have been profitable and compensated
much for the lateness of payments by the Crown. Its value
as a check on who was travelling was such that in 1637 the
government issued instructions to check abuses that were
arising, such as the hire of horses by persons pretending to
be on State service, neglect to pay for horse hire, and the
riding of horses beyond the next stage, or too fast, or with too
great a load.[15]

Most postmasters must have been innkeepers. William
Hugessen, postmaster of Dover, writing to Secretary Windebank
in 1636 declared that he kept 'the most convenient and fairest
house betwixt London and Dover, and where ambassadors
generally lodge'. He wished to renounce his postmastership in
favour of 'his tenant in the house called the Greyhound of
Dover'.[16] The fact that the tenant, Edward Whetstone, wanted
the postmastership at a time when his landlord was owed £400
for his services, is an indication of the value of the position
regardless of the delays in payment.

A Royal Proclamation of 31 July 1635 confirmed that horse
hire from postmasters was to be charged at the traditional rate
of 2½d. a mile, both for travellers and the conveyance of mail,
or an express. At this period, however, the present measured
statute mile was not universally used, and there was no work
of reference listing milages between towns on the main roads
of the realm. This omission was not rectified until 1675 when
John Ogilby published his *Britannia*. Kentish miles were recognised to be longer than those in most other areas of the

country. In 1633, on the section of the Dover Road between Canterbury and Dover, the charge for horse hire was 3d. a mile to compensate for this. The postmaster of Dover and others who hired horses appear to have taken advantage of this to try and increase their earnings, by setting up posts at each statute mile, though still charging 3d. a mile. They declared the distance to be 15¼ miles, and thus at 3d. a mile claimed 3s. 9d. for the journey, an increase of 9d. on their previous charge. Edward Whetstone was summoned to answer for their action before the Privy Council in London.[17]

In July 1637 the royal postal service was limited to letters on His Majesty's business, and those subscribed by persons connected with the government. This no doubt encouraged the considerable number of private enterprise posts that operated, some of which were encouraged by municipal authorities. *The Carriers Cosmography*, published in 1637, lists 'the footpost of Canterbury who doth come every Wednesday and Saturday to the sign of the two neck'd Swanne at Somers key neere Billingsgate'. Two years before this Edward Ranger, who was described as 'foot post of Dover' was examined by Sir John Bankes, the Attorney-General regarding the convenance of sums of silver and gold amounting to several thousand pounds to Dover. Ranger is still listed as the Dover footpost in 1649.[18] A footpost also existed between Sandwich and London by way of Deal. In 1662 the mayor and corporation of this town petitioned against the post office monopoly mentioning John Axtell 'our ancient messenger . . . who hath faithfully served this Corporation ever since one thousand six hundred, thirty four'.[19] He appears to have carried citizens' as well as corporation letters. Such footposts must have been slow, infrequent and led to duplication of routes.

Apart from the postmasters appointed for the various stages along the Dover Road, official postmasters existed at Deal and Sandwich. These appointments appear to have been made in connection with the despatch of orders to, and the receiving of information from, ships sheltering in the safe anchorage of the Downs before passing the North Foreland into the Thames Estuary. The duties of the Sandwich postmaster specifically mention carrying 'his Majesty's letters aboard his Majesty's ships' and building 'warning fires on shore' in this connection.

Captain J. Penington of the *Swiftsure*, writing from the Downs
in May 1637 was full of praise for Robert Smith, the deputy
postmaster of Deal

> a careful diligent man in sending away the King's packets, and in
> making fires at all hours both night and day, to give us notice when
> he receives any for us; and further he keeps good hoys which his
> predecessor never did.[20]

Letters were despatched and received as and when necessary
connecting with regular posts at Dover. There also appears to
have been some use made of the Rye Road with a postmaster
at Rye itself. In September 1640 the Mayor of Rye wrote to
'Secretary Windibank' stating that George Edge, the postmaster,
'has been very dilligent in carrying the King's packet and
furnishing passengers with good horses at reasonable prices'.[21]
As it was forbidden for mail entering the country to use Rye as
a post of entry the work of the postmaster was probably to
deal with the occasional express, and to provide post horses
for travellers.

Despite his appointment for life, Witherings' tenure of office
was not to last long. In 1637 Sir John Coke and Sir Francis
Windebank, the two Secretaries of State, took over the inland
posts, and in 1640 Witherings lost the foreign posts also. His
ambitious plans had probably not fulfilled their expectation
and the financial troubles of Charles I demanded every possible
reduction in government expenditure. Sir John Coke, Witherings'
patron, had retired as Secretary of State in 1640 and his successor
proved less sympathetic. The office of Postmaster was transferred in 1640 to Philip Burlamachi and he retained this until
the outbreak of the Civil War in 1642.[22]

This conflict ended any immediate hopes for the improvement of the service. Kent reluctantly sided with Parliament
during the Civil War, and this ensured the continuance of the
line of communication between the continent and London.
Already before the outbreak of hostilities there is some
evidence of a deterioration in the service. Robert Reade writing
to his cousin Thomas Windebank from Paris in March 1641
informed him 'the posts are of late in very much disorder'.
As late as February 1642 the postmasters on the Dover Road
were deemed loyal enough to obey warrants issued by the
King's Secretary of State to provide horses, but this route was

soon to be closed to the King. By the end of 1643 only certain postmasters of the Western Road could be relied upon, and James Hicks, formerly Clerk of the Chester Road, was employed by the King to collect such sums of money as were due, and to establish fresh routes to replace those leading to London. A new route to France was essential, and this was established using vessels from Weymouth to Cherbourg.[23] Meanwhile in Kent the County Committee, responsible to Parliament for the general administration of the area, was making payment to the postmasters, and the account books of Charles Bowles, their treasurer, show sums amounting to £109 paid to Committee postmasters between January 1644 and June 1645.[24]

In the troubled times that followed the end of the First Civil War it was more necessary than ever for the Commonwealth to keep a check on travellers. In 1650 orders were given that vessels for Holland should take no further passengers once they had passed Gravesend, where all passengers, including those with passes, were to be searched. Passengers boarding at Gravesend were to use only the public landing stairs 'that so there may be a better watch kept, and account taken of all persons and things that shall go on board or ashore'. Evelyn, the diarist, posting down the Dover Road in August 1650 was closely questioned by soldiers at Canterbury.[25] Letters, especially those from royalist exiles, were opened as a matter of policy. In May 1649 a warrant was issued by the Council of State to Captain Edward Saxby ordering him to search all foreign posts and 'seize the letters of persons suspected of holding correspondence with the enemy'. Such letters were to be brought to the Council of State for examination. Royalist exiles were aware that this was happening, and as a consequence wrote with caution. Jane Short, a royalist, writing from London in February 1650 to her brother, Thomas Short, at La Rochelle indicated her suspicions:

> The jealousies of the times are great and consequently the danger of writing; all packets are stopped, which is the reason you do not hear from me.

Sir Edward Nicholas, writing from the Hague in December 1654, declared the local postmaster to be 'a very rogue, and a creature of Cromwell's and I believe he sends to a correspondent postmaster in England all letters that go hence to any English in London'. Such suspicions were fully justified, for the Post Office Act of 1657 declared quite openly that one of its main purposes was the detection of seditious intrigues 'the intelligence whereof cannot well be communicated but by letter escript'.[26]

On the other hand the Commonwealth authorities were justified in suspecting that plots and disaffection were being aided by postal communication. Attempts were made in August 1656 to undermine the loyalty of the navy by sending to a number of captains commanding ships in the Downs pamphlets 'abusive and derisive to the present Government'. Authority was given to the Deputy Governor of Dover Castle and the Mayor of Dover to open all letters sent to seamen in order that 'the authors and dispensers of such villainous pamphlets may be discovered'. Royalists organised their own 'postmasters' to smuggle correspondence into Britain. Colonel John Bamfield, one of the spies working for John Thurloe, the Secretary of State, uncovered one such route in June 1657. A Calais merchant by the name of Baron was acting as postmaster and was receiving weekly packets from England and making regular return despatches. Realising that inland letters were not searched as closely as the foreign mails, he was using the crews of packet boats to carry letters to Dover and arranging for them to be posted there.[27]

At such times reliable postmasters were vital to the Commonwealth, and a careful watch was kept for treasonable correspondence. After the 1648 rebellion, orders were given that 'in the Cinq Ports a close watch' was to be 'maintained upon the activities of searchers, postmasters and members of corporations'. Justices were instructed to take 'strict account of all strangers', attend to the posts along Watling Street, and examine persons who spoke 'contemptuous words' against the government. The Sandwich footpost was dismissed after complaints from Thomas Rainsbrowe from Dover Castle, that if he were not replaced he would complain to parliament. Edward Ranger, the Dover footpost, was similarly dismissed by the mayor and justices of that town. In both cases their political allegiance was felt to be suspect. Postmasters also found themselves replaced. In August 1651 Nicholas Whetstone, then postmaster of Deal, was summoned to London, and the Navy Committee ordered to appoint 'some well-affected person' in his place, and also to see that 'faithful' men were provided as postmasters at other stages on the road between London and the Downs. John Whetstone, the postmaster of Dover, and probably a relation, was also dismissed for expressing 'much disaffection to the Parliament and commonwealth'.[28]

During the Commonwealth no complaints are heard of arrears of pay, so common in the reign of Charles I. In July 1652 the Navy Committee ordered the Naval Commissioners 'to make out a bill for nine months wages extra from 25 Dec. last to 29 Sept. next' for the postmasters on the Dover Road. Amongst those mentioned by name were Michael Marsh of Southwark and Sam Woodley of Sittingbourne. Their duties at his time were stated to be heavy and the cost of feed for horses high.

Apart from the routes to Dover and Deal no other posts within the county appear to have been regularly used at this period. Orders were, however, issued in May 1653 for a new post route to be established from Dover to Portsmouth because in time of war it was thought to be useful 'for the Publique service especially for the Navy'. At the same meeting of the Council of State the ruling against illegal letter conveyance was repeated, and inland letters both private and public were 'to be managed only by those authorised by the State'.[29]

Since 1642 the head of the Post Office had been Edmond Prideaux, but in 1653 he was replaced by John Manley who agreed to pay £10,000 per annum for the privilege of being able to enjoy a monopoly of the carriage of mail for his own benefit. His appointment was followed the next year by an Ordinance of the Commonwealth government designed to regularise postal arrangements. This obliged Manley 'to keep one or more Foreign Packet Boats to be weekly employed for the Foreign Posts, as hath been formerly used and accustomed'. This would suggest a poorer service than that envisaged by Witherings in 1633 which provided for three foreign posts a week. Certain new routes were specified including that from Portsmouth to Dover, authorised a year previously. The 1654 Ordinance also laid down postage rates and certain general regulations. Single letters conveyed under 80 miles were charged 2d., beyond that in England and Wales 3d., to Scotland 4d. and to Ireland 6d. Postboys were required to convey the mails at seven m.p.h. from 1 April to 30 September, and five m.p.h. for the remainder of the year. Postmasters were to maintain one horse especially to convey the mails, and the changing of horses at each stage was not to delay the mails for more than 30 minutes. Four good horses in addition were to be kept for those persons authorised by the State to ride post. Such posters were to pay 3d. a mile hire. Freedom from military and jury service was granted to postmasters and two of their servants. The conveyance of letters was declared a government monopoly, and post horses could only be provided to travellers by postmasters. Penalties were laid down for persons who abused the regulations.[30]

John Manley's term of office was short, for in 1655, the Secretary of State, John Thurloe, assumed control, emphasising the importance of the post to intelligence. Revised instructions to postmasters regarding the transmission of mails were issued in this year.[31] They were to keep a book in which to list the day and time of the arrival of mails as a check on speed of transit, and were to have '2 bags lined with cotton' for the conveyance of letters. Mails were to be carried to London three times a week and a label provided on which the time at each stage was to be entered. Postmasters were to keep ledgers in which all letters were to be entered and accounts were to be settled every three months. With the permission of local magistrates, horses might be requisitioned for public service. On the basis of the regulations issued in 1654 and 1655 the first Post Office Act was framed in 1657. This, re-enacted in 1660, was to form the basis for the regulation of postal affairs for the next half century.

Chapter 2

THE KENTISH POSTS, 1660-1784

THE RESTORATION of the Stuarts in 1660 heralded a period of expansion in postal traffic. Henry Bishop who took over the farm of the posts in 1660 was obliged to pay £21,500 annually for it, compared with £10,000 paid by Thurloe. National postal receipts were, however, rising year by year.[1] In 1688 they were just under £90,000, but by 1693 had risen to £116,000. The increased revenue was derived mainly from an improved network of postal routes and a more frequent service. Postal rates were similar to those prevailing during the Commonwealth. Effective attempts were made to enforce the royal monopoly.[2]

By 1724 the total revenue had risen to £178,071 on which the Treasury received a net profit of £96,339. Postal rates had, however, been increased in 1711 by amounts varying from a third to a half. Taking this into account, it might suggest that nationally the number of letters conveyed was beginning to level off. After 1724 revenue did not rise again until 1735, and thereafter it increased steeply.

1746	..	.. ..	£201,460
1772	..	.. ..	£309,997
1781	..	.. ..	£417,634

The rise from 1770 was particularly steep. Profits, however, tended to lag behind the rise in revenue, and the 1724 level was not reached again until 1762. Thereafter they rose steeply to a figure of £161,944 in 1767. A peak of £173,188 was reached in 1774, followed by a decline, and after 1783 a further rise.[3]

Figures on which revenue for Kentish post offices for the period 1660 to 1784 can be calculated are somewhat incomplete.

As postmasters were liable to fall into arrears, in some cases quite substantially, with payments to the Post Office, figures of amounts remitted to London are not reliable enough on which to base calculations. A much more accurate estimate can be obtained by extracting from the Post Office ledgers, where these exist, figures of the amounts due in postage on letters sent to the various post towns, as this was seldom pre-paid.

During the five-year period 30 June 1672 to 20 June 1677, when Colonel Whitley was in charge of the operation of the Post Office the revenue from Kentish offices rose considerably.[4] For the offices on the Dover Road and branches between 1672/3 and 1678/9 the rise amounted to 26.6 per cent., or 3.8 per cent. per annum. On the newly-opened route to Rye and Hastings the rises were even more spectacular, amounting to no less than 291.3 per cent., or just over 41.6 per cent. per annum. This rate of rise appears to have levelled out, and in the six years that followed, up to 1685, the revenue on the Dover Road rose only 5.6 per cent., and that on the Rye Road 9 per cent. No further figures exist on which calculations can be based until 1720.[5] Over the 35-year period 1685 to 1720, the increase from the Dover Road was 66.7 per cent., averaging out at a little under 2 per cent. per annum, though the Rye Road was still doing well with a rise of 255.5 per cent., or 7.3 per cent. per annum. Rates of postage had, however (as already noted), risen in 1711, and taking this into account the figures for the Dover Road show a poor rate of growth. The superior increase for the Rye Road may be attributable to the cancellation of farms on certain traffic on this road in 1711.[6] In the decade 1720-30 postal traffic from the Kentish offices appears to have fallen off. It rose again in the period 1730-40, but fell again in the next decade. Overall, the period 1720-50 showed a fall in revenue.[7]

This falling-off in revenue appears difficult to explain, as the population of Kent was probably rising in the first half of the 18th century. It has been estimated at 155,694 in 1701 and 168,679 by 1751.[8] Although figures for national postal revenue over these years show a general stagnation,[9] Kentish revenue does not even appear to have been maintaining its proportion of this national revenue.

TABLE I

Comparison of Kentish and National Postal Revenue, 1730–1750

	1730			1740			1750		
	£	s.	d.	£	s.	d.	£	s.	d.
Dover Road	2,524	19	8	2,996	14	2	2,834	5	11
Rye Road	886	5	2	831	4	8	856	16	11
Totals	3,411	4	10	3,827	18	10	3,691	2	10[10]
National revenue of the Post Office	£178,817			£194,197			£207,490[11]		
Percentage of Kentish[12] gross revenue to national gross revenue	1.91%			1,91%			1.86%		

The pattern of a sharp rise in the period to 1680, followed
by a more modest rise to 1720 and stagnation to 1750 corres-
ponds to a fair degree with the facts concerning the expansion
of postal routes within the county. In the period following
1660, and especially the decade 1670–80, not only was confidence established in the regularity and efficiency of the royal
postal system, but the number of offices and routes in Kent
greatly expanded.[13] A further expansion in postal routes
followed the cancellation of the farms in 1711[14] but, after this,
stagnation appears to have set in.

After 1750 revenue from Kentish offices appears to have
jumped ahead again paralleling a similar national rise. Although
detailed figures for each office are not known, the gross revenue
from all Kentish offices in the year ending 5 April 1785 is
available. At £8,961 5s. 11d. it represented an increase of
106 per cent. over the period of nearly 35 years since 1750, or
over 3 per cent. per annum. The postage collected in 1784
within the county represented 2.1 per cent. of the national
postal revenue, appreciably higher in proportion than that
for the period 1730–50. Some of the increase may have come

from an improvement in the revenue collected from bye-post letters in the county. Bye-post letters were those passing from one office to another on the same post road and therefore not passing through London. These were difficult to account for. It was not until 1765 that attempts systematically to enforce payment were made on the Rye and Dover Roads. In this year it was suggested that returns of such letters should be made under oath by the postmasters, accounts of such letters should be kept at the Bye and Cross Post Office, and salaries paid to the postmasters for this duty. In 1784 bye-post revenue was £872 or 9.7 per cent. of the total county revenue.[15] In other parts of the country effective means of accounting for bye- and cross-post letters had been taken much earlier in the century.

Postal Routes

(b) The Dover Road and its branches

The stages on the Dover Road by 1660 were already well established, and no attempt was made to alter them. A description of the post route issued in 1667 lists them as:

	Post Miles from London	Cuntry Miles from London
Lond		
Southwarke		
Dartford	14	12
Rochester	14	12
Sittingbourne	12	11
Canterbury	15	12
Dover	15	12[16]

The same pattern is repeated in later surveys with minor exceptions. London is substituted for Southwark as the despatching point and the importance of this office declined. A new office was in existence at Ospringe in 1673, but this must have been short-lived.[17]

Most post routes had three despatches a week, leaving London on Tuesday, Thursday and Saturday. This pattern was well established in 1673 when Richard Blome issued his *Britannia,* and was to continue till the end of the next century

LONDON

DARTFORD ● ─── ● GRAVESEND

BROMLEY ●

WEST MALLING ●

SEVENOAKS ●

MAIDSTONE ●

TONBRIDGE ●

Tunbridge Wells ●

Cranbr

STONECROUCH ●

Hurst Green ●

Battle

Hastin

──·──·── Routes Operated Regularly Prior to 1660
━━━━━━ Routes Operated by the Post Office Opened After 1660
·············· Routes Under Farm

KENTISH POST ROUTES c.1700

QUEENBOROUGH

MARGATE

RNE

FAVERSHAM

CANTERBURY

WINGHAM

SANDWICH

DEAL

ASHFORD

DOVER

Folkestone

Hythe

den

Tenterden

New Romney

Lydd

YE

on most roads. The Dover Road, however, from soon after the Restoration enjoyed a six-day service, despite the fact that despatches for the continent were only made up twice a week. The only road that could boast an equally good service was that to Colchester, which had the same frequency in the late 1670s.[18] The service was infinitely better than that which prevailed in the period before 1660.[19]

The Dover Road served the most thickly-populated and most prosperous part of the county, meeting the needs of a number of important towns en route. A number of other towns situated within a short distance of the direct route were served by branches.

At Dartford, the first stage on the Dover Road, a six-mile branch to Gravesend was established. This must have been settled at an early date, and was certainly in existence by 1635. The town was of considerable importance both for its maritime connections and for the garrison of the fort established here. At Gravesend ships were given final customs clearance on their passage from London, and it was at this point that many travellers to the continent, who had come from London in the ferry, hired horses for their journey through Kent. This 'great ferry' had been noted by Taylor in his *Carrier's Cosmography,* and had been used by Evelyn, the diarist, on his journeys to the continent, and the extent of its use had amazed Defoe.[20] The hire of post horses was profitable to the postmaster of Gravesend, and at times no salary was paid to him. In 1678 the postmaster was paying the Post Office £5 a year. Usually the postmaster of Dartford appears to have been responsible for the conveyance of mails to and from Gravesend. The town enjoyed a six-day post, the same frequency as the Dover Road.[21]

From Rochester, the next stage on the road, an important branch extended to Maidstone, the administrative centre of West Kent, which was soon to be the hub of an extensive network of branches itself. The exact date of the opening of the Maidstone office is not known. It was not included in the 1667 survey of post roads, but appeared in an official table of post towns two years later. The lateness in opening the Maidstone office may be due to the fact that the Mayor and Corporation had in 1641 set up an unofficial three-day post to London, and had for nearly a century before this been employing official corporation messengers.[22] Maidstone was considered to be a good base for the distribution of letters to the neighbouring areas. On his appointment as postmaster at Maidstone in 1673, Mr. Maplesden received a letter from Colonel Whitley, the administrator of the Post Office then in farm to Lord Arlington, exhorting him:

> to send more Letters from thence and Branch out to the neighbouring Townes, within 5 or 6 miles of you, and allsoe have Ashford in your thoughts.

The post was sent daily, except Sunday, and it was assumed that the postboy who collected the mail at Rochester would arrive in time to deliver Maidstone letters to the London-bound postboy. Mr. Maplesden was not, however, very co-operative in this respect as it would mean both dispatching the mail from Maidstone at about 2 am. to make the connection, and then a wait of several hours at Rochester for the postboy from London. In December 1674 Colonel Whitley was complaining of letters being allowed to 'lye 12 or 14 howers' at Rochester, having arrived too late to connect with the postboy to London.[23]

An extension was settled from Maidstone through Lenham to Ashford in 1675. Previously letters for Lenham had been sent to Maidstone, and those for Ashford to Canterbury. By June 1675 Colonel Whitley had made arrangements for the delivery of letters to Lenham three times weekly. At Lenham the Ashford letters were to be taken over by Robert Lott, who had been appointed postmaster of Ashford. The first mail to these new offices was forwarded from London on 7 June 1675. Ashford continued as a post town,. but Lenham had the status of a post town for only a brief period following its opening in 1677.[24]

To the west of Maidstone were the small towns of Aylesford and West Malling. Colonel Whitley was of the opinion that a further branch from Maidstone might serve them, and on 17 June 1676 he wrote to Mr. Maplesden asking him to make arrangements to set up such a route. No record exists, however, of an office being established at either place as early as this, though a service was certainly opened in 1698 from Maidstone three days a week.[25]

Chatham existed as an independent post town from the beginning of the 18th century; previously it had been served from Rochester. The increase in the importance of the naval yards and the population dependent upon them for their livelihood, no doubt brought about the opening of the new office. Already by the 1720s Defoe noted the 'ware-Houses and store-houses for the laying up the naval treasures' as being the largest in the world.[26]

The third stage on the Dover Road was Sittingbourne, from which two branches originated. The most vital of these was the one to the Isle of Sheppey serving the important garrison at Sheerness. This fort commanded the mouth of the River Medway and gave protection to the naval base at Chatham. Already by Defoe's time, outside the fortifications, 'a kind of town, with several streets in it, and inhabitants of several sorts' had arisen. The Sheerness branch served on its way the ancient corporate town of Queenborough, described by Defoe as being 'a miserable, dirty, decay'd, poor, pitiful, fishing town'.[27]

Sheerness, as the civilian population was small, did not easily qualify as a post town. Most of the correspondence was military mail on State service, and in the period from 23 February to 24 December 1675 the Sittingbourne postmaster forwarded no fewer than 272 letters to the garrison by express messenger. By this date Queenborough was already a post town but Major Darell, the commander of the garrison, objected to the need to send a messenger there to collect the mail. Colonel Whitley was loath to meet the expense of the wages of a further postmaster, but on 20 November 1676 he indicated that he was prepared to make such an appointment and allow a salary of £4 per annum, 'the Remaynder (if this will not content him) must be made upp by the Garrison'. The office is listed in 1682 in Thomas Gardiner's *A General Survey of the Post Office,* but was closed in March 1705.[28]

The Queenborough office was opened earlier than that at Sheerness. By August 1673 Colonel Whitley had agreed with a Nicholas Badcock of Queenborough to receive letters at his house and act as postmaster. The Sittingbourne postmaster was to be responsible for the despatch of letters three times weekly and the Sheerness garrison were expected to collect their mail from Queenborough. The office is listed in the 1677 version of Thomas Gardiner's *A General Survey of the Post Office* but is missing from the 1682 revised text. Also the office is not mentioned in the post office accounts covering the period from this date up to 1705. This would suggest that the Sheerness office was the only one functioning on the Isle of Sheppey at this period. Queenborough appears once more in the lists of post towns after the closure of the Sheerness office in 1705. An alternative explanation might be that the office was retained at Queenborough, but referred to as the Sheerness office.[29]

The other branch listed under Sittingbourne was that to Faversham. This office was not open at the time of the 1667 survey but must have opened soon after, as it is mentioned in Richard Blome's *Britannia* (1673), and letters from Colonel Whitley to the postmaster give no indication that this was anything but a well-established office of several years standing.

A regular official post to Deal, Sandwich and Margate followed soon after the Restoration. Henry Bishop, advertising that he had taken over the farm of the Post Office in 1660, declared that he had 'at his great expense settled many new posts in several new roads and by roads where heretofore no posts have ever been'. The first of these new posts he listed was 'unto the city of Canterbury, Sandwich, Deal and the Downs'. The private footposts that previously served this area were quickly suppressed. The list of stages on the Dover Road compiled in 1667 shows the entry:

from Canterbury to Deale ..	..	..	6
from Canterbury to Sandwich	..	..	8
from Canterbury to Margate	..	..	14[30]

It would seem unlikely, however, that three separate routes were operated from Canterbury, as the 'tree' showing the postal routes in Thomas Gardiner's survey 10 years later shows only one route from Canterbury leading to Sandwich and at that point splitting into two. The Deal postmaster, or a contractor based on Deal, was responsible for the mail between this town and Canterbury via Sandwich, while the Margate letters were left at Sandwich and taken on by a separate postboy. Deal had a particular importance because of the need to provide for letters to and from shipping in the Downs, but neither Margate nor Sandwich were places of any great importance. Defoe comments upon the use of Margate for the export of Thanet grain to the London market but dismisses Sandwich as 'an old, decay'd poor miserable town'. An additional office at Wingham between Canterbury and Sandwich was opened in 1698, but its limited importance is reflected in the £2 per annum salary offered.[31]

Some provision must have been made for the towns on the coast between Dover and Rye, but no official post office appears to have been set up until the second decade of the 18th century, when Romney, Folkestone and Hythe appear in the accounts for the year ending 25 March 1718. It is probable that before this mail came via Rye. Edward Hall, the Rye postmaster, farmed the posts and branches of the Rye Road south of Tonbridge, and in the declared accounts of the Post Office for the year 1702-3 'Lyd, New Romney, Hythe and Folkestone' are mentioned in the list of places in his farm. The farm ended in 1711.[32]

An additional post office was established at Chislehurst probably in the late 1760s, but from the start this was officially referred to as the Footscray office. The bag of letters appears to have been left with a turnpike gate-keeper on the New Cross Turnpike and collected from him by the postmaster.[33]

The London to Dover road, as befits its importance, appears to have been maintained in a reasonable state of repair. The road avoided the deep clays of the Weald and was passable even in periods of heavy rainfall and in winter. Ogilby writing in 1675 declared it to be 'in general a very good and well-beaten Road, as any in the Kingdom; chiefly Chalk and Gravelly, and none better provided for conveniency of Entertainment.' Celia Fiennes in 1697 declared the route from Canterbury to Dover to be 'a good Road'.[34] This was before any turnpike trusts were operative on the route. By 1750 the whole of the distance between London and Canterbury had been turnpiked with the exception of a small section between Harbledon and Boughton-under-Blean which was maintained by the county. An Act authorising the turnpiking of the section from Dover to Barham Downs was passed in 1753.[35]

(b) The Rye Road and its branches

The Rye Road was of much less importance than that to Dover. By the reign of Charles II the port of Rye was declining rapidly, and the long Anglo-French tariff war that began in 1678 had cripped its foreign trade. The hinterland served by the port could not provide sufficient export cargoes to warrant the heavy cost of maintenance. By 1677 the greatest low water depth in the harbour was three fathoms, and in 1698 a report by the Admiralty Surveyors declared it to be 'in no case proper for a safe harbour to be resorted to, nor capable to be improved by any tolerable charge'. A year earlier Celia Fiennes described the harbour as 'a great tract of land on either side that is chock'd up with sand, which formerly was a good haven for shipps'.[36]

A postmaster existed at Rye in 1640 but probably no regular official post operated as early as this. Henry Bishop included Rye in his list of 'new posts' when he took over the farm of the Post Office in 1660. The Rye Road was included in the surveys of the post roads issued in November 1666, and in the next year, with three stages:

Chipstead ..	..	..	..	..	20 miles
Stonecrouch[37]	..	..	..	..	22 miles
Rye ..	..	..	..	..	23 miles

The stages were thus at nearly double the distance of those on the Dover Road, and indeed most other roads in the country. This probably resulted in a slower speed of transmission. It is significant that neither of the intermediate stages were places of any size or importance, and they must have been picked merely because they happened to be convenient distances on the road. From these stages a number of towns on and off the road could be served. A list of post towns issued in July 1669, suggested that Chipstead was the office for mail destined for Sevenoaks, Otford, Reigate, and Croydon; Stonecrouch for Lewes, Cranbrook, and East Grinstead; and Rye for Winchelsea, Battle, Hastings, Hailsham, and Pevensey. The distances involved are in many cases considerable and the need to collect mail at such distances inconvenient, unless local carriers provided an unofficial service.[38]

Gardiner's survey of 1677 repeats the three stages of the earlier surveys, and states that the post operated twice weekly. Evidence from the Letter Books and Cash Books maintained by Colonel Whitley from 1672 onwards indicate that post-masters were appointed at both Sevenoaks and Tonbridge at this time. The Sevenoaks office was established in June 1676 and Chipstead ceased to act as a post town at this time. The Tonbridge office was in existence in 1672, but its actual date of opening is unknown. A further office was opened at Bromley in 1678, no doubt because of the very considerable length of the first stage. On the lower part of the road, just inside the Sussex border, Lamberhurst appears to have had some form of receiver of letters appointed as early as the 1670s, but he was accountable to the postmaster at Chipstead for money received. Hastings is listed in 1677 as having a post-master, but is not included in the 1682 list, and it is possible that it was then under the farm of the Rye postmaster.[39]

Tunbridge Wells, which was responsible for much of the revenue on this road, was served by the postmaster of Tonbridge, who certainly had his main office at Tunbridge Wells by the middle of the 18th century, employing a deputy to manage the less important Tonbridge correspondence. The value that Colonel Whitley placed on the letters to and from Tunbridge Wells during the season is shown by his instructions to Mr. Carter, the Tonbridge postmaster on 10th July 1673:

> I have ordered the Mailes to goe from hence sooner then ordnary, that the Letters may be at Tunbridge, early in the morning where-fore faille not to be there ready to receive them, and then make all possible hast with them, to the Wells, that the Gentry, may have them before they goe to their Lodgings.

As early as this date a Mr. Miles, 'confectioner on the Walke' was acting as receiver of letters, and the Tonbridge postmaster was instructed to collect the letters from him every post day. Postal traffic developed rapidly. In 1672 the value of postage collected on letters sent to Tonbridge during July and August was only £2 7s. 3d., but only four years later it was £36 14s. 6d. The high rate for these two months must have been entirely due to visitors to the spa, as the winter figures for December and January were only 17s. 10d. in 1672 and £3 4s. 6d. in 1676.[40] Celia Fiennes, apart from noting the 'shopps full of all sorts of toys, silver, china, milliners and all sorts of curious wooden ware', mentions the 'post house' and the postal arrangements. The spa continued to flourish in the next century and its popularity was commented upon by Defoe amongst others.[41]

The main road to Hastings and Rye avoids Tunbridge Wells, but there is evidence that by 1755 the town was being served by the Hastings to London postboy. During the Tunbridge Wells season, the town received a daily post, Sundays excepted, though before 1687 there was no post on Monday either. Eighteenth-century almanacks indicate that this daily post ran from Midsummer Day to Michaelmas.[42]

A number of other small towns was served from this road. Cranbrook, Tenterden, Biddenden, Battle, and Hurst Green are listed in 1704 in the places served under the farm of Edward Hall, the Rye postmaster. Hurst Green and Battle were on the main road to Hastings, but the other towns would have needed branches to serve them. In the accounts for the year ending 25 March 1718 Cranbrook, Biddenden, Tenterden, and Hurst Green are listed as post towns all with salaried postmasters. Ten years later the offices of Battle, Stonecrouch, Cranbrook Biddenden, and Tenterden are shown in the accounts grouped together under the Hastings postmaster, having obviously lost their status as independent post towns. By the 1770s Battle and Stonecrouch are once more listed as post towns, but Tenterden, Biddenden, and Cranbrook are listed together, presumably under the Tenterden postmaster. By 1781 Cranbrook had its own postmaster again, but Biddenden was still under the Tenterden postmaster.[43]

The Rye and Hastings Road traversed the clay vales of Kent and Sussex where good stone for road construction was not always easy to obtain. The importance of the summer traffic to Tunbridge Wells ensured a reasonable standard of attention to the road as far as this town, but beyond it conditions were very different. Ogilby commented that especially beyond Tonbridge the way was 'not altogether commendable'. Celia Fiennes, writing two decades later, confirms the words of Ogilby about the road south of Tonbridge.

During the second half of the 17th century the first turnpike acts were passed by parliament, allowing tolls to be collected from road users' to ensure adequate standards of road maintenance. The first turnpike act for the county of Kent was in respect of the section of the Rye Road between Sevenoaks and Woodsgate (Pembury), with a branch road from Tonbridge to Tunbridge Wells. The Act, which was passed in 1709, described this section of the road as 'very ruinous and impassible insomuch that it is become very dangerous'.[44] In 1749 the section from Sevenoaks to Farnborough was turnpiked, thus ensuring a road of reasonable quality from London to Tunbridge Wells.

Beyond Tonbridge, however, the Hastings and Rye roads still had a bad reputation. The first turnpike act relating to this section was passed in 1741 and covered the road from Woodsgate (Pembury) to Flimwell, and in 1753 a further Act gave powers to turnpike the section from Flimwell to Hastings which was described as:

> so ruinous and deep in the Winter Season, that neither Carriages, nor persons travelling on horseback can pass without Danger and Difficulty.[45]

Despite efforts at improvement, travellers still complained of defects. Horace Walpole found that he was completely unable to hire horses at Tonbridge, and the only person who had them available would not supply them for fear that they would be injured because of the condition of the road. He next tried Tunbridge Wells, and after waiting half a day, he managed to to obtain horses and set out for Hastings. He found, however, that beyond Lamberhurst 'the roads grew bad beyond all badness, the night dark beyond all darkness and our guide frightened beyond all frightfulness'.[46] The postboy responsible for the carriage of mail from Hastings to London was in December 1755 accused of delay. In defence he stated that:

> this is a road which is very subject to Delays on Account of the water which cannot be avoided, and Except this Accident of the water, being now and then impassible, am sure you'll find no Delay on my part.[47]

The section of the London to Rye road beyond Flimwell was not turnpiked until 1762.[48] Parish roads were seldom repaired to the standard of the turnpikes and often merited such descriptions as 'generally rough, hard and narrow' or 'sad deep unpassable . . . when much raine has fallen'.[49] Over such roads the mail had to be conveyed.

The Speed of Conveyance and Rates of Postage

The speed of transit for the mails had been laid down in the first half of the 17th century as seven miles an hour in summer and five miles an hour in winter, and no attempt was made to improve on these official speeds until the end of the 18th century. A writer in 1681 proudly announced:

> This conveyance by Post is done in so short a time by night as well as by day, that every 24 hours, the Post goes 120 Miles, and in five days an answer of a letter may be had from a Place 300 Miles distant from the Writer.[50]

Despite the fact that the official speed ought not to have taxed the capabilities of the postboys, complaints of delay were numerous. Most of them appear to have been due to nothing other than slackness, such as the failure of postboys to keep time or postmasters to provide fresh mounts immediately. Failure of the mail to reach London on time meant delay to the General Letter Office staff, and was far from popular. Writing to Jeremiah Masterson, the Canterbury postmaster, on 1 January 1674, Colonel Whitley complained:

> Of late there is not a day in the week but the officers waited 2 or 3 houres Extraordinary for the Kentish Maile; and this Day they attended of it; till 8 A Clock att night.

On this occasion the mail appeared to have taken 14 hours to travel from Canterbury to Sittingbourne. In March 1676 Colonel Whitley complained to the Dartford Postmaster that mails were taking 18 to 20 hours to reach London from Dover, and the next year all the postmasters on the Dover Road received a further remonstration:

> There is no Roade in England that gives us the like trouble of waiting that yours does: although you have almost double the time allowed you that others have.

Apart from complaints from the staff of the Letter Office in London, Colonel Whitley was liable to be criticised by the chief officers of state on the one hand and merchants on the other, if the valuable continental mails off the Dover Road were late. On 12 August 1676 he wrote to all the postmasters on the Dover Road pointing out the embarrassment caused to him by foreign couriers delivering despatches in London many hours before those for the British government. He suspected the Dover postmaster of being more concerned with providing passengers from the packet boats with horses than the postboy. Merchants were equally concerned for early news from the continent that might afford them commercial advantage, and Colonel Whitley claimed that delay:

> Causes a Rumor among the Marchants & persons concerned, that I am scarce able to stay in my House.[51]

Mail should have been despatched from Dover in the afternoon between the hours of 5 and 6 o'clock, and according to the regulations reach London early the next morning. At times it did not arrive until nearly nightfall. Delays could be caused by late departure from Dover or Deal, because the inland mail was held awaiting the arrival of the packet with the continental letters in the case of Dover, or mail from a ship calling at the Downs from a foreign destination in the case of Deal. Instructions were given that the mail was not to be delayed more than 15 minutes because of this, and if necessary express messengers should be sent after the postboy with the foreign mail when it landed. Thomas Gardiner writing in 1677 complained:

> We find also a great mischief and disorder in allowing to the Kent Road three hours beyond their usuall dispatches; which from Dover was constantly at 3 in the afternoon, now at six (under pretence of staying for Shipp Letters or the Forrain Mailes). This packet being generally of itself not more than 40 or 50 shillings in value hinders the going abroad of all other our letters, and the delivering them before exchange time.[52]

Much of the delay must have been due to neglect. At times it took the mail 18 to 20 hours to complete the journey, while delays of three to four hours were not unusual. Often it was one stage that caused the trouble. Complaints that the mail took six hours from Canterbury to Rochester and six hours from Rochester to Dartford are recorded. The Sittingbourne to Rochester stage was particularly bad, the times recorded for this being five hours on one occasion, six hours on another and even 12 hours. In April 1674 the postboy had to wait two or three hours at Sittingbourne for a horse to be produced, the postmaster's servant 'being in Bedd'. Of 25 cases of complaint of late delivery for the Dover Road in Colonel Whitley's Letter Books for the years 1672 to 1677, 10 were for the winter months January to March, when the roads were probably at their worst. Four, however, occur in the summer months of July, August, and September. The Dover Road was not unique, and other roads had similar delays recorded for them. The Rye Road appears to have been freer from complaint. The amount of correspondence from the post-masters on this road was less, and the mail did not contain important overseas letters or despatches, so there would be less need to hold the delivery of other letters from the General Letter Office in London if the Rye postboy had not arrived on time.[53]

The method of keeping such negligence in check and ascertaining the culprit was by means of a label attached to the mail, on which postmasters at each stage were required to indicate the time at which the mail reached them. General instructions and information to postmasters could also be written on the labels. In February 1674 Colonel Whitley used this method to request postmasters on the Dover Road to submit claims to him for the carriage of express letters and extraordinary duty. Labels could be lost. To ensure that loss was not used to cover up for delay and negligence, instructions were issued that mails received without a label were to be reported, and the times recorded on a plain piece of paper. Postboys losing labels were to be punished. There was still the temptation to put the wrong time on the label to cover up for shortcomings. A servant of Robert Vivian, the Rochester postmaster, was guilty of this fraud in May 1674, altering the time of receipt from 12 noon to 1 pm. In October of the same year the Sittingbourne postmaster recorded the time of arrival of a mail from Rochester as 5 am., whereas the postboy had arrived at 3 am.[54]

A number of these post labels have survived,[55] and confirm the statement of contemporary writers on the speed of postal transmission. An analysis of the labels for the conveyance of French or Flemish mails from London to Dover or vice versa reveals the following:

TABLE II

Time taken to convey mails from London to Dover or vice versa, 1667–8

Year	Months	No. of journeys recorded in sufficient detail	No. of hrs. journey completed in					
			14 hrs.	15 hrs.	16 hrs.	17 hrs.	18 hrs.	over 18 hrs.
1667	Jan.-Mar.	6	—	—	—	2	3	1
1667	May-July	4	1	2	1	—	—	—
1668	Feb.–Mar.	15	—	1	2	6	3	3
1668	Aug.–Aug.	34	—	4	7	19	3	1
Total, Jan.-Mar.		21	—	1	2	8	6	4
Total, Apr.-Aug.		38	1	6	8	19	3	1
Totals		59	1	7	10	27	9	5

John Ogilby in 1675 reckoned the measured distance from London to Dover as 71½ miles.[56] The average winter journey time shown by these post labels was 17.7 hours, giving an average speed of 4.1 m.p.h.[57] The summer figures show some improvement on this with an average journey time of 16.3 hours and an average speed of 4.4 m.p.h. Thus even in summer the official winter rate of travelling of five miles per hour was not attained; the official summer speed of seven miles per hour must have seemed an impossible goal. The printed instructions on the post labels of 1667 detail no speed of transit, merely informing both postboy and postmaster that they should 'use all dilligence and expedition in the safe and speedy conveyance of this Mail', and warning them 'not to fail, as you will answer the contrary at your peril'. The 1668 labels[58] have a speed of five miles an hour listed on both those used for summer and winter transmissions.

Postage rates were fixed by the Post Office Act of 1660[59] at 2d. for the first 80 miles and 3d. for longer distances for single letters, i.e., one sheet of paper only. Letters consisting of two sheets were charged double, and those of four sheets or more were charged at four times the basic rate per ounce. The rates applied only to the borders of England and Wales. Rates in addition were charged for carriage in Ireland and Scotland. Each single rate was increased by a penny in 1711,[60] and in 1765[61] cheaper rates were introduced for short journeys. The percentage increases[62] were therefore:

TABLE III

Postal Rate Increases, 1660–1784

	1660	1711	% increase on 1660	1765	% increase on 1660
one stage (approx. 10 miles)	2d.	3d.	50%	1d.	−50%
two stages (approx. 20 miles)	2d.	3d.	50%	2d.	50%
first 80 miles	2d.	3d.	50%	3d.	50%
above 80 miles	3d.	4d.	$33\frac{1}{3}$%	4d.	$33\frac{1}{3}$%

The rate increases of 1711 appear to have been justified both from the need to raise additional revenue to finance the war and also on the basis that prices had risen generally and with them no doubt the cost of operating the service.[63] No attempt was made, however, once hostilities had ceased to reduce rates until 1765 when new rates of 1d. for one stage (about 10 miles) and 2d. for two stages were introduced. These were no doubt brought in because short distance letters were liable to be illegally conveyed by carriers if the lowest Post Office rate was 3d.

Letters were usually received by postmasters without payment, the recipient paying the postage. But in June 1676 a Mr. Butler claimed that the Faversham postmaster refused to accept his letter without payment. This resulted in the Faversham postmaster being informed that 'he ought to leave all men to theire free choyce whether to pay for them or not'. Letters of Members of Parliament during the period that the Houses were in session were carried free of charge, and the Rochester postmaster in July 1673 was ordered to apologise to Mr. Head, the local member, for detaining his letters for the payment of postage.[64]

Apart from the usual despatch of mail regularly on the Dover and Rye roads, it was necessary quite frequently to send individual letters or despatches of great importance that could not be held to the next post with all speed. Expresses were regularly despatched from the Navy Office to Sheerness and the Downs, especially in times of war. Postmasters were expected to retain 'two or three sufficient horses alwayes in readinesse to Carry his Majesties Expresses &c as Occasion shall require'. In May 1673 both King and the fleet were in the vicinity of Rye and the postmasters of Chipstead, Stonecrouch and Rye were authorised by warrant 'to prease horses for his Majesty's Service', and from 15 to 24 May 1673 the post was made daily. A similar situation occurred in June 1676 when the King was at Sheerness and powers to commandeer horses were given to the Sittingbourne postmaster. Express messengers were also used to convey last-minute instructions to ships that had sailed from London, but were due to call in at the Downs or Dover. Colonel Whitley wrote on 5 May 1677 to James Houseman, the Dover Packet Contractor and Agent:

> The enclosed to Mrs Churchill, requires extraordinary hast & care, shee went yesterday in the Cleaveland Yacht; if she be not at Dover, hyer a Boate expresse, to bring it to her at Calais.[65]

Payment from the government for expresses was however slow in coming. Thomas Gardiner wrote in 1677:

> Another discouragement to Postmasters is the hard work of carrying the King's Expresses for nothing. It being a matter almost equall to it, of not being paid in severall yeares; never untill such time as money is to be had from the King's Eschequer.

The only answer that Colonel Whitley received in January 1674 from the Navy Office on enquiry into money for James Houseman's expresses was that 'itt will be paid in Course'. In January 1677 Robert Gascoigne, the Sittingbourne postmaster, was paid for the expresses despatched in 1674, but no payment was received for his 1675 expresses. In June 1674 Henry Finch, the Sandwich postmaster, was waiting for his payment for expresses up to Christmas 1673 but 'not yet is one penny Rec'd.'.[66]

Even in the regular posts, special care had to be taken in order that offence was not given to the military forces of the Crown, or to Members of Parliament by any slackness. The postal route to Dover was of particular value in time of war, especially at periods when British forces were campaigning on continent. In April 1676 postmasters on both the Harwich and Dover Roads were informed that:

> It is his Majesty's pleasure, that all possible Dispatch should be made with the Mailes (especially Foraign Mailes) during the Season that the Armies are in the field.

A few months later in February 1677, instructions were issued to postmasters on all roads to use utmost diligence to see that mails were not delayed during the sitting of Parliament. They were also to see that those Members who hired post horses were provided with good animals and equipment, and not charged for their franked letters.

The post did not convey parcels, for these were left to the many carriers that existed. As letters of one ounce were charged at four times the single rate for a letter, the cost of conveyance of even small parcels would be beyond all reason. Parcels intended for the royal household or senior posal officials were liable to be presented to the postboy for conveyance. The contents were most varied. On 15 April 1676, the postmaster of Deal was sent a letter from Colonel Whitley thanking him for a mullett that he had been informed had been despatched to him by post but had not arrived. Another such gift acknowledged on 20 April was a cheese from the Shrewsbury postmaster. Parcels of lace, purchased on the continent, were sent through the post by foreign postmasters to Colonel Whitley himself. Even boxes for the Secretaries of State might contain other than despatches. The Packet Agent at Dover in November 1675 received instructions to send 'my lord Arlington's Box immediately on Receipt, as I believe, it containes Trouffles for the King, and they will be certainly spoilled by delay.[67]

The Postboys

The postboys who conveyed the mails were not Crown employees, but servants of the postmasters along the route. Every postmaster who contracted to convey the mails provided his own postboy. Riding was often at night and in all weathers, and he had no means of protection from footpads and other highway robbers. The evidence seems to suggest that the sense of loyalty and responsibility was not always as high as could be wished for. No doubt from time to time completely unsuitable men were employed on this work. Most postmasters were innkeepers, and any servant of the household who could be spared was liable to be sent. In November 1672 a delay of three or four hours appears to have occurred on the stage between Sittingbourne and Rochester, and this was blamed on the fact that the Sittingbourne post-master employed 'a Couple of Young Boyes; very Unfitt for your business'. Drunkenness of postboys whilst engaged in their duties was not uncommon. On 17 May 1676 the Dover post-master was reprimanded for employing 'carelesse drunken Rouges' as postboys. He was informed that when his postboy arrived at Canterbury:

> he was soe drunk, that he could not speake, & that he is almost alwayes soe, when he comes with your Bag, also that yesterday after the Maile was ready, it was halfe an houre before they could find him, & then (being drunk) he would not carry the Forreign Mailes, but went away without them.

Postboys were directed to deliver letters and also collect them from certain favoured persons who happened to be on their routes. Accusations were made that these postboys demanded excessive amounts in postage and 'with the money received, they may lye gameing, and drinkeing on the way.[68]

Neglect was not always the fault of the postboys, who from time to time must have been provided with poor mounts and worn-out equipment. Between 1672 and 1677 the postmasters of Deal, Canterbury, Rochester, and Dartford were admonished by letter for providing inadequate horses. The hire of horses to travellers was put before the needs of the Post Office. The Canterbury postmasters in September 1677 had only three horses 'and not one of them fitt for the service', while the Dartford postmaster in June 1674 hired his best horses to travellers and provided a mount which the postboy found so weak that he was obliged to walk. The horse died before reaching Rochester. The mounts provided by the Deal post-master were so poor that the mails had to be despatched two hours early in order to reach Canterbury on time. In May 1674 the mails were delayed four hours at Rochester while the ostler went three miles to fetch a horse 'from grass', and when in November of the same year the postmaster's property was seized by the Post Office for debt, the horses were described as 'soe poore, as unworthy of their meate'. The bags for conveying the mails were at times defective. This Colonel Whitley blamed on foreign postmasters, who he claimed kept the sound ones in which he sent the mail and supplied in return worn out ones. In May 1675 he complained to the French postmaster:

> this fortnight wee have received 2 from you without either Seale or Chaine and soe torne and full of holes, that Mr. Houseman was forced to repair them at Dover.

A further letter on the same matter was sent seven days later.[69]

At times the postmasters would not even send one of their own servants at all but gave the bag to a traveller who happened to be going in the right direction. In September 1673 the postmaster of Chipstead, on the Rye Road, was accused of often sending his mail 'by Fishermen & such kinds of people'. In July 1675 the Canterbury postmaster entrusted his mail to 'a Strange Dutch man without a Guide'. The use of such strangers could not have been too uncommon for the Sittingbourne postmaster allowed him to continue with the mail towards Rochester near where he 'Suffered it to be opend, the Secretaryes of State Letters and Pacquetts to be visited, and tore and many letters lost'. Postmasters also used stage coaches to convey mails when short of horses. In December 1674, the Canterbury postmaster hired the horse belonging to the Dover postmaster, which should have conveyed the post to Dover, to a Frenchman, sending the mail on by the next stage coach.[70]

Security of the Mail

Such places as Blackheath near London, and Gads Hill near Rochester on the Dover Road were notorious as the haunts of highwaymen, and extensive records of thefts from the mails might be expected. Colonel Whitley's Letter Books covering the period 1672–77 in fact list only one case of a mail bag being stolen in Kent, and this was by means of a confidence trick, when in April 1674 a person presented himself at the Sandwich post office pretending to be the postboy from Deal. Narcissus Luttrell in his book *A Brief Relation of State Affairs* (September 1678 to April 1714) gives details of the crimes committed in 1693. In this year he listed instances of 39 robberies or attempted robberies; three of these were in Kent. Luttrell mentioned 45 or 46 highwaymen taken during the

year, and under February listed 40 highwaymen and their
haunts. The April entry listed double that number. This suggests
a considerable activity amongst highwaymen at this period.
He mentions no robberies of mails on either the Dover or the
Rye Roads and only three such robberies for the whole country
[London–Harwich twice, and Penzance to Marazion].[71] In the
W. V. Morton collection of postal history documents and
literature at Bruce Castle, Tottenham, are newspaper cuttings
listing mail robberies on the Dover Road in 1712, 1729, 1754,
1758, 1763, and 1767. Of these, four were cases where the
postboy was stopped en route and robbery committed. In two
cases the bags containing the mails were taken and rifled, but
in the other two it was the postboy himself who was robbed
and the mails left strictly alone. Of the remaining two cases one
involved the theft of a bag whilst the postboy's horse was left
unattended, and the other concerned the incitement of postboys to steal banknotes from the post.

Nationally the number of mail robberies does appear to have
increased by the second half of the 18th century, resulting in
the consideration of safer methods of mail transit. In August
1770 the *St. James's Chronicle* reported that:

> Yesterday a Mail Cart of a new Construction was brought to the
> General Post Office in Lombard Street. It is so contrived as to
> prevent the Mail being robbed or carried off for the future; and will
> immediately be made use of.

A rival appeared in the following year, however, invented by a
certain Mr. Moore:

> the body is made of Iron, and so strong that it is thought it will be
> impossible to break it open.

The search for new types of mail cart was by no means at an
end, and in December 1780 a correspondent recommended:

> the making and fixing in each Mail-Cart of a large strong Box, with
> one of the Patent Locks lately recommended by the Police; the keys
> of which should be kept only by the Postmasters of the different
> Towns. This would infallibly prevent future Mail-Robberies.

Mail carts were adopted by the Post Office on main
routes and were in their turn soon to be superseded by mail
coaches, when the condition of the roads and the volume of
passenger traffic warranted their introduction. On all but

local routes, the mails at the end of the 18th century had grown too large for the older type of horse rider to cope with. Horse posts did manage to survive on the Rye Road into the 1770s, however, and in November 1771 William Laslett and Thomas Theobald were accused of stealing the Tonbridge bag from the rider. Laslett was found to be in possession of several banknotes missing from letters contained in this mail, and it was probably the increased despatch of banknotes through the posts which made the robbery of the mails more attractive. The exploit of George and Joseph Watson in robbing the Bristol mail cart on the night of 28 January 1781 with a haul amounting to more than £10,000 pointed to the danger of using this means of transit for banknotes. In February 1782 the Post Office advised persons sending such notes to cut them in two, forwarding the halves by different posts.[72]

Smuggling in the Mails

During the reign of Charles II the Customs became aware of a considerable traffic in small dutiable items through the post. In 1666 a proposal was made to appoint 'persons of discretion and condition' at Canterbury and Rochester 'with power to search the mails, but without delaying the post'. The Post Office fought hard against such proposals, maintaining the sanctity of correspondence from such arbitrary search. It was also pointed out that correspondence for His Majesty and his ministers was conveyed, and this would be put at risk by the action of the searchers. Nevertheless, mails were stopped and searched. In May 1674 the post was searched without warrant at Rochester. The servant of the Rochester postmaster responsible for allowing the search was reprimanded by Colonel Whitley:

> I am much amazed, that soe discreete a person, as you seeme to be, should suffer soe violent a Presumption to be Committed upon his Majesty's Maile, Except he had produced an Especiall Warrant . . . ye Searcher will be sent for Speedily up, and severely punished for his presumption, and made Exemplary to others.

One of the reasons for Colonel Whitley's concern can be noted in his letter of 25 June 1674 to Monsieur de Vallege, his French opposite number, in which he reported the Rochester episode. The mail was evidently stopped and searched because contraband goods were clearly to be seen through holes in the mail bag. Other items of correspondence in the same letter book indicate that Colonel Whitley was himself engaged in smuggling in such goods. After a further incident in June 1675, in which a mail was searched at Sandwich, Colonel Whitley was sufficiently alarmed to write to the Antwerp postmaster advising him to warn his subordinates to refuse all further 'Marchandies (Prohibited or free) in the Mailes', as it would 'probably expose our Mailes to be opened, not onely by the Searchers but by Robbers on the highway'.[73]

A settlement appeared to have been reached late in 1675 when the Commissioners for Customs were informed that:

> for the future no Custom House Officer do presume to break open the mail, but if they know or suspect any prohibited goods to be in the mail, they are to acquaint the Post Master with it who is to assist them in the seizure.

Despite these assurances of co-operation, in May 1679, Joseph Champion, an officer of the customs was complaining that:

> parcels of fine lace are very much suspected to be brought over in the mails from France and Flanders, and that he lately followed the mails to the Post Office and desired to see them opened, but was evilly treated by the officers there.[74]

Chapter 3

KENTISH POSTMASTERS, 1660–1784

LOYAL POSTMASTERS were necessary if the service of the State was effectively to be carried out. During the period of the Commonwealth a number of postmasters suspected of royalist sympathies had been replaced, and in 1660 petitions from all over the country were received from those who asserted that they had been dismissed because of their loyalty to the Crown. For the postmastership of Sittingbourne there were two contenders, Robert Barham, who claimed that he had been dismissed 'for having served in the late King's army', and Richard Gad who was recommended as loyal and fit for the office 'and had been postmaster before the late troubles'. Arthur White, the Gravesend postmaster, although appointed in 1645, claimed that prior to this he had been 'dismissed from service in the Navy for loyalty' and had 'lost much in the Kentish rising of 1648'. In 1663 it was made a ruling that all postmasters within six months should bring a certificate of their conformity to the Church of England on pain of dismissal. Lists of postmasters for this date are unfortunately not known and therefore it is not possible to check if any dismissals did take place. Previous political loyalties were not soon forgotten. When in 1668 a man named Gilpin was being considered as the Sittingbourne postmaster, Sir Thomas Wilson wrote to Sir Joseph Williamson, the Secretary of State, accusing Gilpin of being 'a fanatical and imoral, a former creature of Pride and Sir Mich. Livesay'. Such denunciations were not always based on truth.[1]

The postmaster was not an employee of the Post Office in the same sense as the staff of the General Letter Office in London. He was usually an innkeeper who took the position in order to gain the monopoly right of posting travellers, and to bring custom to his house. He might also contract to supply horses and postboys for the conveyance of the mails. A petition dated 7 March 1660 in favour of the appointment of Robert

Barham as postmaster of Sittingbourne gives his trade as inn-keeper, while Arthur White, postmaster of Gravesend in 1660, had kept in the early 1640s 'an inn at Milton' and was probably still in the same trade. An order of January 1673 forbade the quartering of soldiers on 'any innkeeper, victualler, or any other person who is actually a postmaster, master of a letter office or packet boat'.[2]

Postmasters displayed a sign or notice indicating that they held the appointment. When Robert Lott was made Ashford postmaster in July 1675, he was sent 'a printed paper, which is convenient alsoe for you to hang up in a frame, at your door'. Postmasters were expected to set aside a room for their postal business but this may often have been neglected, to the prejudice of security. In November 1674 the Rochester post-master was taken to task for his neglect of the letters:

> there lyes a great abondance of them scattered aboute your house, especially in your Chamber, and upon the Tester of yr. Bedd.

He was told to:

> sett some Roome a Part to be your office, in which onely you should bring the Mailes open, and Close them, and where you should sort the Letters and Let noe Body come into it, but your self.

In appointing postmasters, the Post Office was at a great disadvantage before 1715, when the first permanent surveyors were appointed. There were no full-time paid Post Office officials outside London, and to fill vacant postmasterships meant relying on people who lived in the locality concerned, and also on certain loyal postmasters. James Neal, the Deal postmaster, was in October 1674 requested to settle the Sandwich and Margate offices:

> I heare from Sandwich, that Mr. Finch is gone into ye Contrey quits his Imployment soe doth his agents in ye Isle of Thanet, and without giveing me the least notice . . . I must desire your assis-tance ernestly desiring you to go imediately to Sandwich and Thanet, and settle ye office in both places.

Negotiations to fill such vacant offices were not always easy, as Colonel Whitley was not generous with the salaries that he was prepared to offer those taking over the offices.[3]

On appointment new postmasters were sent their 'Articles and Bond' which they were obliged to sign and seal in the presence of the minister of the parish and other witnesses. They were also obliged to provide two sureties, who would hold themselves responsible should the postmaster fail to return the sums due to the Post Office. The appointment was only confirmed once these had been received. Cases arose of the reluctance of postmasters to return these documents. Robert Lott, the Ashford postmaster, was appointed in July 1675, but his articles and bond had not been signed and returned in September 1676 despite much urging.[4]

Dismissal of postmasters was usually because of debt. In November 1674 Mr. Masterson, the Canterbury postmaster, was dismissed for this reason. He owed in the region of £100, and as this was not forthcoming, action was taken against his two sureties. One of them, Mr. Curtis, was arrested and placed in prison for his failure to settle Mr. Masterson's debts, as it was thought that he had the ability to pay. Some sureties were more fortunate. In 1689 James Cornwall, described as 'Innholder', and John Andrews, a 'Barber Chururgeon', who were sureties for Richard Gilham, another Canterbury postmaster who had run himself into debt, were discharged because the debts 'would totally ruin' the two men and their families. Daniel Hall, the Gravesend postmaster, was dismissed, had his property sold, and 'his wife and thirteen children then living in the house' were 'turned out of doors & became Objects of Charity'. He blamed his misfortune on the 'Late & Present War' which no doubt reduced the number of travellers to the continent. Despite the money raised from the sale of his property a debt of £108 remained.[5]

The salaries provided for postmasters, especially in the second half of the 17th century, were the subject of bargaining, and a low payment is not necessarily an indication that a post town dealt with a small volume of mail. It may be a reflection of the volume of trade brought to the postmaster in the form of the provision of refreshment, lodgings and horse hire. In 1677 on the Dover Road and its branches no salary was given to the postmasters of Maidstone and Queenborough, while Sittingbourne, Gravesend, and Dartford postmasters actually paid the Post Office for the privilege of having the appointments. The highest salaries on the Road in that year were Deal with £75, Canterbury £50, and Southwark £40, but these figures certainly included payment for the conveyance of mails. On the Rye Road in 1677 only the postmasters at Sevenoaks with £8, and Rye with £15 were allocated a salary. Payment was sometimes made on the basis of a proportion of the postage on letters. At Ashford a fifth of all the postage on letters to and from the town was allowed in lieu of salary when the office opened. In 1677 this amounted to about £8 a year, and to supplement it a salary of £10 per annum was also allowed. This did, however, have to cover the carriage of letters to and from Lenham, three times a week. Postmaster's salaries were paid quarterly, and were listed as a credit against the postmaster's account in the ledgers. Thus we hear nothing of the arrears of postmaster's salaries that existed in the 1630s. The Maidstone salary which up to 1698 was only £10, and in the next century never more than £30 per annum, was supplemented by a two-thirds share of the postage collected on the branch opened in that year from Maidstone to West Malling. In 1699 this alone amounted to £27 14s. 4d., and in the following year had increased to £33 18s. 9d. From 1680 salaries started to rise, but as the figures quoted as salaries often contain amounts paid for such duties as riding work, payment of a local letter carrier, etc., comparisons are not always easy. From 1698 to the 1770s the Canterbury salary was £95, after which it rose steeply; Rochester was paid £50 in 1694, which had risen to £60 by 1711, £70 by 1741, and £100 10s. 0d. by 1771. The Deal salary of £105 paid throughout most of the 18th century was a combination of three former salaries, £45 for the management of the post office, £20 for the riding work, and £40 for the use of boats in connection with the collection of letters from ships calling in at the Downs. These relatively large salaries allocated to important offices may be compared with the £2 per annum salary paid at Wingham from the establishment of the office in 1697 until the end of the century.[6] The general tendency for salaries to rise was a reflection both of the rising volume of postal business and a falling-off in the number of posters at the end of the 18th century with increasing competition from stage coaches.[7]

The monopoly position that the postmaster held of horsing people travelling post and providing them with guides must have been one of the greatest incentives to take an appointment as postmaster. Guides were equipped with a horn which could be sounded as a warning for other travellers to allow room to pass. Those hiring horses from a postmaster were to be sent direct to the house of the postmaster of the next stage, and there to be provided with fresh mounts to ensure their speedy passage. Such a system depended upon the co-operation of the postmasters concerned. In practice the earnings of some postmasters might be affected by the failure of others to co-operate. Both the Sittingbourne and Gravesend postmasters appear to have sent posters direct to each other and ignored the intermediate stage at Rochester. By this means their earnings, based solely on mileage, were increased at the expense of the Rochester postmaster. When tackled about this in May 1674, Robert Gascoigne, the Sittingbourne postmaster, used as his excuse that the Rochester postmaster 'hath noe accommodtion'. In June of the same year he 'horsed three and twenty Passengers with a Guide to Gravesend', and in May the next year was still ignoring repeated pleas to be just to the Rochester postmaster. In November of the following year complaints were made against Mr. Price, the Gravesend postmaster, for sending posters direct to Sittingbourne.

At Canterbury the complaint was of a different nature Here posters were being sent by both the Deal and Dover postmasters to innkeepers other than the postmaster. Such actions threatened the livelihood of the Canterbury postmaster, and thus the despatch of mails, which were to some extent subsidised from the earnings from posters. Colonel Whitley appears to have been able to take little action in such cases. He could only hope that the actions of the offending postmaster would give him the chance to put pressure on him for some negligence of his official duty. This is what happened in May 1675, when the Sittingbourne postmaster was informed:

> by your Illegal procedding in horsing them through to Gravesend you have now Rune your self into a snare, for last week you sent a Foreign Maile by Strangers . . . who delivered it not at the Posthouse there, but to the man who lives at the house, where Mrs Skyllman formerly did.

Mrs. Skyllman was a former postmistress of Rochester. It was for the latter offence that he threatened to call Mr. Gascoigne to London 'to answer your Misdemeanors before the King and Counsell', not for the posting irregularity.[8]

By the Post Office Act of 1660 the postmasters' monopoly of posting men with guide and horn was renewed. If, as seems likely, this trade was valuable, it is not to be wondered at that illegal posting, by the hire of post horses and guides by people who were not postmasters, was practised. In May 1667 Edward Whetstone, the Canterbury postmaster, was complaining to Sir Joseph Williamson that:

> the men who keep horses in the town daily horse out-landish men with or without guides, and if guides come from Sittingbourne or Dover will pull them off their horses, before the writer's face.

In November 1674, a certain Mr. Parker of Deal, another illegal hirer of post horses was told to stop his activities. The letter probably had little effect, for in February of the next year, James Neal, the postmaster, was advised to take legal action against Parker for damages. Mr. Laming, the Margate postmaster, had the same trouble in February 1678. Again the same solution was advised. Legal action was an uncertain remedy, for it was not illegal merely to hire out horses. In his advice to Laming, Colonel Whitley stated the position clearly:

> if they horse then with a horne and guide you have the Advantage of them Butt if they do but Accommodate them as ordinary Travellers, the Law can take no holde of them.

The difficulty in dealing with such practices led at least one postmaster to take the law into his own hands. Robert Glover, the Dartford postmaster, in December 1675 was accused of pulling from their horses a number of Frenchmen travelling to London, and forcing them to hire from him. Unfortunately for the postmaster one of the travellers was the son of the French ambassador.[9]

The system of riding post had its supporters, such as Thomas Delawne who in 1681 wrote:

> Moreover if any Gentleman desire to ride Post, to any Principal Town of England, Post-horses are always in readiness.

The Post Office Act of 1660 was, however, more realistic, and one clause permitted posters to hire horses anywhere, if the postmaster could not produce them within half an hour.

In 1662 Jack Verney was forced to delay his journey four hours at Canterbury as he found difficulty in obtaining a horse, and in May 1673 a gentleman riding post in the service of Prince Rupert was obliged to wait two hours for a horse. Rates for posters had been laid down in the Act of 1660 as 3d. a mile for the hire of the horse, and 4d. a mile extra if a guide was required. Accusations of excessive charges being made at Canterbury are recorded in September 1673. The importance to the State of many of the travellers riding post must have ensured a generally satisfactory service, and Colonel Whitley was at pains to warn postmasters to 'be carefull to accomodate all those that shall ride Post, with good Horses & Furniture'.[10]

Postmasters had to face a growing threat to the posting traffic from coaches. Before 1660 this was only serious in the area near to London. By 1647 coaches were being used between Gravesend and Rochester in connection with the long ferry from London, and on 21 July that year the Corporation of Gravesend made an order restricting the plying as hackney-men of foreigners and strangers 'within the towns of Gravesend and Milton'.[11] After the Restoration, long-distance coaches began to be established on the main roads, and in the 1683 edition of *Angliae Notitia or the Present State of England*, Chamberlayne was able to boast:

> There is of note such a admirable commodiousness for both men and women to travel from London to the principal towns in the country, that the like hath not been known in the world.[12]

Opposition from the postmasters and other interested parties resulted in petitions urging the government to control the growth of coaching. William Warde, a solicitor representing several English towns, presented one such petition in 1671 to Lord Arlington, urging that such stage coaches be restricted to:

> one a week, by special licence to each of the long stages as Dover, Portsmouth, Norwich, York, Chester, Bristol and Exeter, which would be to the joy of thousands of subjects; since . . . the complaints of the country have exceedingly increased, the coaches growing more numerous and their servants more abusive to those that petitioned against them.

Some postmasters attempted to take direct action against those who preferred coaching to posting. In September 1674 it was complained that Mr. Curtis, the Canterbury postmaster, deliberately hindered a man from taking 'a place in a coach that lay in the Inn', and forced him to hire horses even though the traveller suffered from ill health. In July 1676 Mr. Bevis, the Rochester postmaster, went further and arrested some coachmen, presumably for a violation of what he supposed to be his monopoly. He received an official rebuke for his action:

> the Law prohibits any person, (except a Post Mr.) to horse Posters with horne & a guide, But I have not read that it forbids any man to Hire his Horse whither he will, nor a Coach to Carry Passengers.

By the mid-18th century coach services were becoming frequent and regular. An advertisement of 1747 announced, 'The Rochester, Sittingbourne, Ospringe, Canterbury, Dover and Deal Fying Stage-Coach from the Spread-Eagle Inn, Gracechurch Street, London'. This coach left every Tuesday, Thursday and Saturday, completing the journey in one and a half days. Private coaches could be hired that would reach Dover or Deal in a day, while Rochester was served by a separate daily service.[13]

Apart from the earnings from posting travellers and the care of their needs, and the salary received from the Post Office, certain other perquisites and advantages existed for the postmaster. Some of the more substantial and suitably-placed postmasters had the chance to farm branches, or bye letters.[14] Before the appointment of the first Post Office Surveyors in 1715, checks on the operation of the posts away from London were difficult to make, and it was often preferable to accept a fixed rent from a farmer. Thomas Gardiner writing in 1677 stated that bye letters:

> having therefore no check on them, were wholly swallowed up by the Postmasters or Servants. And although we have found out a method . . . in some measure to prevent that fraud, and to draw into the office 2 or 300 pounds per annum, yet it seems not perfectly effectual to oppose their confederacy.[15]

On 4 December 1673 Colonel Whitley wrote to Henry Finch, the Sandwich postmaster, asking him for an account of his bye letters which 'must needs be Considerable'. He asked for a daily account of them on the letter bill 'as you are obliged to doe, or if you see good you shall Farme them, as many other

Post masters do'. In June of the following year Colonel Whitley informed Nicholas Badcock, the Queenborough postmaster, that if Robert Gascoigne, the Sittingbourne postmaster:

> doth not perform his Business as he ought to doe, I will farme the letters of Quinborough Sheerness &c to you, if you have a desire of Undertaking.

It is, however, on the Rye Road that farming developed to its greatest extent in South-east England. On 21 February 1673 Colonel Whitley offered the whole of the road[16] to Robert Hall of Rye. This was probably because of the low yield from the Rye Road which in the year ending 30 June 1673 produced only £43 12s. 11d., compared with £978 16s. 7d. for the Dover Road. There is no evidence to suggest that the offer was taken up, and it is not until 1686 that there is any clear evidence of farming on this road. In the year ending 25 March 1687 Mr. Hall paid £75 10s. 0d. for a farm of the southern end of the road, and this section was thereafter permanently in farm until 1711. Treasury accounts for the year ending 25 March 1705 declared the extent of the farm to be:

> all the letters to and from London to and from Hastings, Battle, Cranbrooke, Bidenden, Tenterden, Appledore, Hurst Green, Lyd New Romney, Hythe and Folkestone.

Robert Hall was appointed postmaster of Rye in 1677. The farm appears to have been taken over by Edward Hall whose name appears in the 1705 accounts. He was described in 1706 as being of 'Hastings Co., Sussex', and in 1707, and subsequently as 'Edward Hall of Rye'.[17]

The other farm of the Rye Road was that listed in the Post Office General Accounts for the year ending 25 March 1687 as 'Edward Kent of Tunbridg £5'. The farm had been taken over by Robert Vernon by 1690 at the same rate. On 29 September 1692 John Brett took over at the greatly increased rent of £32, which by 1696 was down again to £5. The farm in all probability was that of the branch from Tonbridge to Tunbridge Wells, but in the Treasury accounts for the year ending 25 March 1705, the farm is listed as 'John Brett of Tunbridge, Farmer of all letters to and from several towns in Cos. Kent and Sussex', and for this and the subsequent year the rent was steeply increased to £330 per year. Clearly for these two

years the farm must have included a much greater area than
that immediately surrounding Tonbridge. The farm came to
an end in 1711. The origin of this farm may perhaps be seen
in the extra charge of 2d. made by the Tonbridge postmaster
in 1677 for the carriage of letters from this post town to
Tunbridge Wells, where no official post office existed at this
stage. Colonel Whitley was of the opinion that this charge
was excessive and when Celia Fiennes visited Tunbridge Wells
20 years later the additional fee charged was a penny.[18]

Local delivery charges occurred in other towns and were
regarded as the perquisites of the postmaster responsible for
running the service. The letter carriers employed on such services were employees of the local postmaster. No legal sanction
existed for such extra charges, but where this was clearly an
additional service carried out at the postmaster's own expense,
such additions were usually paid without complaint. An exception were the officers of the naval dockyard at Chatham who on
26 April 1669 wrote to the Navy Commissioners concerning
the Rochester postmaster:

> few letters come in due time, and when they do, it is with an abuse
> of his own innovation, obliging us to pay a penny for each we
> receive upon the Kings service or otherwise for carriage from
> Rochester hither.

On certain routes postboys might deliver letters to houses on
their direct route and for this service an additional fee was often
demanded. In August 1675 the postboys delivering foreign
letters that had come from Dover to Canterbury were not only
demanding an additional penny above the postage, but if this
was refused told the intending recipient that the letters would
be thrown into a ditch. It cannot be ascertained if such charges
were authorised by the postmaster of Dover, but at the same
time the Canterbury postmaster was accused of demanding
an extra penny on foreign letters put into his office. The Dover
and Canterbury postmasters may have had an agreement over
this additional charge. That such profits from local delivery
could be substantial there is no doubt. In 1768 the salary
of the Footscray postmaster was stated to be £34, but his
profits from local delivery fees was estimated to be £156 per
annum.[19]

The result of a legal decision in 1772 was a direct threat to the postmasters' earnings from these delivery fees. Prior to this year the postmaster of Sandwich had charged an extra delivery fee on letters from London, but had delivered those from the cross and bye posts free. His attempt to charge on all letters led to an action being taken against him in the King's Bench seeking a declaration that under the terms of the Post Office Act of 1711 letters ought to be delivered to addresses at no extra cost. The declaration was obtained and as a result the Post Office felt itself obliged to provide free delivery in all post towns that had at some time in the past enjoyed this privilege. It was realised that this would cause a considerable loss of income to many postmasters 'the greater part of whom are at present much underpaid'. To establish the point that such fees were legal in towns that had never enjoyed free delivery, a ruling was sought in 1774 from the Court of the King's Bench in the case of Hungerford in Berkshire where it had never been 'the usage to deliver the Letters without a Recompense'. The result was the opposite to that hoped for, Mr. Justice Willis declaring that:

> the Post Office have no right to demand this Penny within the Particular District of the Post Town where this office is held, and to be sure it is much more unreasonable that they should demand it in so little a Town as Hungerford and not in London and Westminster.

The Post Office was obliged to bow to this ruling, but it was not until 1835 that free delivery was granted in all post towns.

A further perquisite enjoyed by postmasters was the free delivery of their own letters, a privilege also enjoyed by government officials and members of parliament. The growing abuse of this concession in the 18th century, when those with the franking privilege frequently endorsed the letters of friends, relations and even business houses for free carriage, resulted in tighter restrictions being imposed.

In the 1670s letters in reasonable quantity appear to have passed free, whether official or not, but Colonel Whitley made it clear to the Dover postmaster in September 1675 when he complained that he had been charged postage, that this was a privilege and not a right. In July 1676 Mr. Lodge, the Deal postmaster, was rebuked for sending lists of ships in the Downs

regularly to the Navy Office and Customs House in London
without payment. It was pointed out that free delivery covered
only single letters concerned with the postmaster's private
affairs and not business correspondence for which he received
an additional income.[20]

Postmasters were also entitled to one or two free gazettes
or newspapers each week. For some offices in the 1670s these
were the only form of payment. It was contended in London
that these gazettes were valuable to the innkeepers who became
postmasters as they brought custom to their houses. Thomas
Gardiner writing about the postmasters declared:

> they receive a reciprocall benefitt with the Clerkes in the General
> Office, by receiving Gazettes free of postage, wherewith they advan-
> tage themselves in the common trade of selling drink.

Gazettes are known to have been received by several Kentish
postmasters in the 1670s.[21]

To ensure that postmasters were not distracted from attend-
ing to the speedy passage of the mails, they were excused from
jury service and the need of quartering soldiers. A certificate
could be obtained through the Post Office in London to be
shown to quartering officers, but some postmasters who were
slow in applying for such an exemption certificate had soldiers
billetted on them. In June 1673, the second year of the Third
Dutch War, Robert Vivian, the Rochester postmaster, had
soldiers quartered on him. He was advised to make the best of
it until the soldiers were drawn away from Blackheath, and then
his protection from quartering would be sent. In August of the
same year Robert Glover, the Dartford postmaster, was in a
similar plight, and the next month the Faversham postmaster
was writing for protection from quartering. This was sent to
him with the advice:

> I must entreate you to use it discreetly . . . in time of necessity
> (when the Towne is over-burthened) to take Some into your house:
> rather than give generall Discontent.[22]

The most important duty of the postmaster was the conveyance of mails. Not every postmaster was responsible for riding
work, but the majority were. In some cases this conveyance
was performed by a contractor who was not a postmaster,
but in the late 17th century this was rare. In 1673 separate

riding duty and office salaries are listed for Canterbury, Dover and Deal. In the case of Deal three separate salaries were involved, riding work, office, and boat duty. These might well be in the hands of the same man, however, and in June 1674 James Neal, who was the contractor for all three, refused to listen to a suggestion that the duties should be split and that he should retain the riding duty only. The rate paid for riding work was at first open to bargaining, but by 1682 was sufficiently fixed for Thomas Gardiner to write:

> The sallaries of Postmasters may be observed to have fallen into a sort of method by giving 20 shillings a year to every mile riding, and soe proportionably not respecting the difference of their labour.[23]

Whether the postmaster undertook riding work or not, he would be responsible for letters to addressees in his area and the collection of the postage due. The General Post Office in London kept a ledger in which the amounts of postage due on letters were recorded, and accounts were rendered monthly. The difficulty of making remittances to London was realised and, apart from the monthly statement, quarterly ones were also sent. Postmasters were allowed to return for credit letters that they had been unable to deliver or those that had been refused. The postmaster's quarterly salary was credited to the account and the postmaster merely withdrew postage money to this amount. Thomas Gardiner was of the opinion that three months was too long a period between remittances as 'Postmasters have failed with great sums in their hands'. To convey their remittances to London postmasters were obliged to use the good offices of fellow citizens visiting the city, or use carriers. The Sandwich postmaster in January 1697 used a hoy to carry his remittance to London. On 18 November 1696, it had been decreed that remittances to government departments must in future be made in milled coinage; the old broad pieces, which were easily clipped, could only be accepted on the basis of weight. One month's grace was allowed, but the Sandwich postmaster did not meet this deadline. The remittance, which he claimed had been accepted for postage before 18 November, amounted to £55 3s. 6d., but taken on the basis of weight it was worth only £30 11s. 6d. The postmaster petitioned to be allowed the full face value of the coins, and this was allowed by the Treasury in November 1700 on the basis that 'the notice was but short and it was difficult to meet with any safer conveyance so as to bring it up in due time'.[24]

Before the appointment of the first permanent Post Office Surveyors in 1715, the central administration in London had no direct means of supervising the working of the service in the provinces. The usual method was to work through existing postmasters. When, in June 1674, the Canterbury postmaster was in debt for a considerable sum in respect of money collected for postages, it was the Dover postmaster, James Houseman, who was asked to go and collect the money 'or Sufficient Security if it were safe (I meane well Secured)'. Mr. Bevis, the Rochester postmaster, was made responsible for the branch to Maidstone and Ashford. In March 1677 Colonel Whitley wrote to him with regard to the neglect of the Ashford postmaster:

> this haveing bin recomended to your Care, I thought you would have have had Eye upon the manageing of it, and not have suffered it to have come to this Confusion . . . I must desire you to take order about the managing of that businesse, until we can put things in a better Posture, and alsoe to enquire for some honest person that will take it upon him.

In September of the previous year, he was considering placing the Gravesend branch also under the control of the Rochester postmaster.[25]

The postmasters, employed by a department of the government, were also expected to provide news of local events that might have a bearing on the security and welfare of the nation. This was particularly important in the case of postmasters situated on the Channel coast. Deal was of significance in this respect because the Downs was often the first place of call for ships coming up the Channel from overseas ports. On 15 December 1674 James Neal, the Deal Postmaster, was ordered:

> to send to Mr. Secretary Coventry, an Exact dayly List, and if any thing Extraordinary happen, give him an Accompt of it, the like I Expect, for my owne Informacion—I will Endeavour to get you a Gratuity from Mr. Secretary.

Not only was the government interested in such information, but also the London merchants, who expected the officials of the Post Office to be able to supply it. On 8 December 1674, when writing to the Deal postmaster, Colonel Whitley disclosed that 'severall Marchants were very Inquisitive after the shipp on the Goodwyn'. One merchant, 'a very Considerable Person', had received the information from Mr. Lodge, a former postmaster at Deal, 'and admired that my Agent should be silent in soe important a matter he spoke it with sharpeness and Reflextion both on you and me'.[26]

Postmasters were expected actively to encourage people to send their letters by means of the Post Office, especially where new branches were established. To publicise the new post to Ashford, the postboy was to 'give notice by his horne, at his comeing in, and alsoe by Rideing a little in the Streets before he returnes, that people may know when to bring theire Lrs. to the Office'. Such publicity was needed to woo letters away from carriers who had previously taken them in default of a regular post. In August 1675 Robert Lott, the Ashford postmaster, was neglecting his duties, and not providing a regular service three days a week. His excuse was the small amount of mail and the continued use of carriers by the inhabitants to convey their letters. It was pointed out that the only way effectively to counter this was to provide a superior service, 'for people must use them, if they have not a Regular Post'.

Successive Acts of Parliament and Royal Proclamations had emphasised the monopoly position of the Post Office as a carrier of letters. It was easier to decree a monopoly than to enforce it. There was a long tradition of private and municipal enterprise in this field, the proprietors of which were reluctant to abandon their efforts. The Corporation of Sandwich fought to retain what they considered as their ancient right to employ their own letter carrier, John Axtell, for their own and the citizens' letters. On 29 August 1662 the Mayor and Corporation petitioned for his retention after seeking legal advice, and in April 1674 he was still operating some form of service from Sandwich and probably carried letters, though the Town Clerk of Sandwich claimed he was a carrier and conveyed parcels only.[27]

Kent had a considerable network of carriers who regularly made their weekly journey to London. John Taylor in his book *The Carriers Cosmographie* (1637) indicated that Tonbridge, Sevenoaks, Staplehurst, Marden, Pembury, Hawkhurst,

Brenchley, Tenterden, Penshurst, Cranbrook, Benenden, Goudhurst, Chiddingstone, Dover, Sandwich, Canterbury, Biddenden,
Westerham, and Wrotham all enjoyed a weekly carrier service
to London. Any of these carriers could have been a conveyer
of letters, especially if the Post Office failed to provide an
adequate service. Colonel Whitley realised that the best way to
deal with the threat from carriers was to provide a faster and
more frequent service. The postboy riding at about five miles
an hour, and carrying the mail at least twice weekly was more
than a match for the carrier's cart. The improved turnpike
roads, which resulted in faster and more regular coach services
in the second half of the 18th century, posed a new threat to
the Post Office monopoly of mail conveyance.

In North and East Kent, coastal shipping could be another
illegal carrier of mail. The volume of such shipping must have
been considerable. In 1683, the port of Faversham alone sent
316 cargoes to London, and this total with the exception of
Newcastle, was the highest that year from any English port.
Daniel Defoe commented upon this trade:

> from these last three towns, Queenborough, Milton and Feversham,
> the fish market at Billingsgate is supply'd . . . from hence also are
> sent by water to London great quantities of fruit.

A little further along the coast Defoe noted the 'vast quantity of Corn' shipped from Margate. When Mr. Laming was
appointed postmaster at Margate in October 1674 he was
instructed 'to hinder the Hoys, wch Carry abundance of Letters
from that Place'. In June 1676 Robert Gascoigne, the Sittingbourne postmaster, was informed that the poor service provided
by Mr. Price, from whom he took over the conveyance of mail
to Queenborough, resulted in letters being sent 'by carriers,
Watermen &c.'. Nearer London the watermen who conveyed
passengers to towns on the Kent bank as far down stream as
Gravesend and Milton were another source of lost letters.[28]

The efficiency of the service in the period following 1660 is
not easy to assess. One Restoration writer declared that the
neglect of the postmasters had 'bin very prejuditiall to the
office of late both as to the Irish Mailes, and the Inland and
must be mended'. The fact that before 1715 there was little
if any supervision at a local level was a serious hindrance. In

cases of bad management, a postmaster could be summoned to London to explain his neglects. On 10 October 1667 Sir John Bennet wrote to Lord Arlington requesting:

> a warrant and a messenger to fetch Arthur Bracker deputy post-master at Rochester and Henry Rouse, deputy postmaster at Dover, as the whole mail was miscarried and only two or three loose bags are brought to the office, with letters so wet and abused that they can hardly be recovered.

Such warrants were issued and messengers were sent to escort the offending postmasters to London. Arthur White, the Graves-end postmaster, was taken into custody by one of them in 1670 'for neglect in the execution of his office'. White wrote to Lord Arlington expressing his sorrow and pleading for release. During the period 1672 to 1677 when Colonel Whitley was in charge of the administration of the posts, several postmasters were threatened with similar action. Such a course was not lightly taken as it would leave a vital link in a main post road without a postmaster. Nor was it always easy to find a replace-ment immediately. From November 1673 to April 1674 Colonel Whitley was obliged to complain to the Sittingbourne postmaster of his neglects on three occasions, and on 4 April 1674 informed him that he would:

> dispose of your Imployment to another, that would be more Carefull in itt, but am now Resolved (Since you Continue your Neglects) in good Earnest to Doe itt, I will allso acquinte my Ld Arlington with your Mis demeanors, that you may be Sent for to answer them here, before King and Councell.

Two years and 10 complaining letters later, Mr. Gascoigne was still the Sittingbourne postmaster.[29]

The service provided, for the most part, must have satisfied the public. The number of letters carried and the Post Office profits rose steadily. The pattern of postal routes and branches on the two Kentish roads had been established by 1680, and with minor changes was to continue for a further century. The postboy with his portmanteau of letters continued at his steady pace to serve the towns of Kent. The blast of his horn was a familiar sound on the road. While the Post Office con-tinued in its old ways, however, change was stirring around it. The stage coach that overtook the postboy on the way was the herald of a period of reform in the Post Office, fitting it better to serve a changing Britain.

Chapter Four

EXPANSION AND CHANGE, 1784-1840

ALTHOUGH NATIONAL postal revenue, as also that for the county of Kent, had greatly increased since the end of the 17th century, the pattern of postal routes had continued with little change during the 18th century. Since the taking over of the farms in September 1711[1] few significant alterations had occurred. Postal traffic was still limited to the two post roads to Dover and Deal on the one hand, Rye and Hastings on the other, and a limited number of branches to towns off these roads. No cross post route yet connected the two post roads at any point. The work of Ralph Allen in expanding the cross post routes in other parts of England did not apply to Kent.[2] Villages, except those of the main postal routes, were nor served at all, unless private arrangements were made to collect letters from the nearest post town.

By 1840, however, there were few villages in the whole county that were not served by an official post. This expansion of postal routes was brought about in large measure under fifth clause and penny post regulations,[3] but also on most of the existing post roads the frequency of service was increased until deliveries and collections were made on all days except Sunday.

The expansion of postal facilities in the county in this way would suggest an increase in postal revenue over the period, and, as similar facilities were provided in other counties in Britain, this ought to be parallel to a similar national increase. In 1783, the year before John Palmer placed the first mail coach on the Bath Road, the national postal revenue stood at £398,624, expenses were £238,999, and the net profit £159,625. The revenue had been rising steadily throughout the century as also had costs. The profits had not risen at such a spectacular pace. Already by 1727 they stood at £100,889 and the next year reached £104,665. They did not top the £100,000 mark again until 1764. After 1784, in part due to

58

Palmer's mail coach system but much more to the considerable increase in postal rates, profits rose sharply. By 1797 they had increased to £513,350; the expenses were only £178,266, appreciably lower than in 1783. By 1806 profits had doubled at £1,119,429, though expenses had risen to £457,686. A peak profit of £1,619,196 was reached in 1816, expenses being £704,639, also a peak. Thereafter both profits and expenses flattened out. It was 1837 before profits rose above £1,600,000 again.[4] It is important to compare these national figures with those for the county of Kent, though these are only available for the years ending 5 April 1785, 25 January 1801, and 25 January 1836. Such comparisons as can be made are set out in Table IV.

Calculating trends on the basis of such limited figures is a doubtful procedure, but they seem to suggest a percentage increase in postal revenue for the county greater than that of the nation as a whole was achieved between 1785 and 1800. This was also a period when the percentage rise in population for Kent also appears to have been above the national figure.[5] It is possible that the increased postal traffic may have been most pronounced in the last decade of the 18th century when the military activity within the county may have been a factor. The increase between 1800 and 1835 was smaller than the national average. Over this period the population of Kent was keeping pace with the national increase with from 3.5 per cent. to 3.6 per cent. of the total population of England and Wales. Much of the Kentish increase would have been in the areas near to London, and thus would not generate substantial additional revenue for the General Post System. The county was not affected to any great extent by industrialisation, and military traffic would have fallen off sharply after the end of the Napoleonic Wars in 1815. Over the whole period 1784 to 1835 the national increase in gross revenue from the posts was 460 per cent., the Kentish increase 422 per cent.[6]

The high rate of profitability of the national postal service was a reflection of a government policy that regarded the Post Office as a source of revenue rather than a service to benefit the public. The postal services in Kent must have contributed to this profitability. Figures, if ever calculated on a county basis, do not exist except in one instance. For the year ending

TABLE IV

Growth of Postal Revenue, 1784-1835

	1784	1800	1835
National Postal Revenue	£420,101	£1,084,000	£2,353,340
Increase in Revenue		£663,809	£1,269,340
Percentage Increase in Revenue		158%	117.1%
Revenue—All Kentish Offices	£8,083 14s. 8d.	£30,631 19s. 10d.	£43,441 15s. 3d.
Increase in Revenue		£22,543 5s. 2d.	£12,810
Percentage Increase in Revenue		279.8%	41.8%
Kentish Revenue as a Percentage of National Revenue..	2.1%	2.9%	1.85%

Sources: Howard Robinson, *Britain's Post Offices* (1953), Appendix II, p. 283; P.O.R. Post 1/12/297; Post 3/18, 3/19, 3/24, 3/25.

5 April 1785 postal revenue for the county was £8,088 14s. 8d., whereas salaries and riding work were £1,555 3s. 4d., leaving a nett profit of £6,533 11s. 4d., or 80.8 per cent. Bye-post revenue for this year was £872 11s. 3d., against which salaries of £105 had to be set. The national nett profit percentage for the same period was 51.8 per cent.[7]

Rates of growth in postal traffic within the county differed from period to period and from town to town. Such movements are difficult to trace with accuracy because detailed figures of postal traffic are available for only 1784, 1789, 1800 and 1835, and these cannot be directly compared because of changes in postal rates. Between 1784 and 1835 there were five increases in domestic rates of postage, but these were not made on an even percentage basis. Between these two dates the General Post rate for a letter from Dartford to London only increased from 3d. to 4d. (33.3 per cent), but a letter from London to Margate rose from 3d. to 8d., a rise of 166.6 per cent. Thus, in Table V, not only has the rise in postal revenue been indicated for each town, but also the rise in the rate for letters between that post town and London. It might be objected that all letters were not sent to or from London, and this is certainly true. There is nonetheless evidence that a large proportion of Kentish postal traffic was with London. A detailed, office by office return of letters posted in the week commencing 15 January 1838 showed that well over half of the letters posted at Kentish offices were addressed to London.[8]

From the figures of national and county revenue quoted[9] there is evidence of a considerable increase in revenue in the period up to 1800 and a much smaller increase in the four decades that followed. Revenue was being boosted in the period up to 1800 by a number of factors. These were:

1. An increase in the postal network and the frequency of service.[10]

2. Improved speed of transit and efficiency due to the introduction of 1784 of the mail coach, and the extended use of mail carts.[11]

3. Military traffic as a consequence of the Napoleonic Wars.[12]

TABLE V

Amounts of Postage Debited to Kentish Post Offices, 1750–1835

Office	1750	1784	% increase per annum	1789	% increase	% increase in postage rate to London	1800	% increase	% increase in postage rate to London	1835	% increase	% increase in postage rate to London
Dartford	£112	£171	53%*	£250	32%	100%	£776	210%	50%	£1,350	74%	33.3%
Gravesend	£123	£303	146%†	£397	31%	50%	£1,000	152%	33.3%	£1,848	85%	50%
Rochester	£254	£543	114%†	£644	19%	50%	£1,824	183%	33.3%	£1,837	1%	50%
Chatham	£301	£1,241	312%	£947	-24%	None	£2,267	139%	33.3%	£2,887	27%	50%
Maidstone	£290	£696	104%	£954	36%	33.3%	£2,424	154%	25%	£5,016	107%	60%
West Malling	£51											
Ashford	£125	£128	2%	£168	31%	33.3%	£670	298%	25%	£1,047	56%	60%
Sittingbourne	£82	£126	54%	£181	44%	33.3%	£504	178%	25%	£1,179	134%	40%
Queenborough	£93	£484	420%	£278	-51%	33.3%	£214	922%	25%	£211	-1%	40%
Sheerness							£2,627		25%	£1,046	-60%	40%
Faversham	£112	£230	105%	£337	47%	33.3%	£821	144%	25%	£1,002	57%	40%
Canterbury	£475	£762	60%	£899	18%	33.3%	£2,795	211%	25%	£4,384	75%	60%
Dover	£252	£597	137%	£714	19%	33.3%	£2,067	179%	50%	£3,067	208%	33.3%
Wingham	£35	£35	—	£58	66%	33.3%	£149	157%	50%	£459	-70%	33.3%
Deal	£148	£638	331%	£421	-34%	33.3%	£2,398	470%	50%	£717	6%	33.3%
Sandwich	£284	£480	218%	£620	-29%	33.3%	£527	-18%	50%	£561	40%	33.3%
Margate	£35	£422	294%	£713	69%	33.3%	£1,553	118%	50%	£2,170	46%	33.3%
Folkestone	£33	£138	30%	£150	9%	33.3%	£542	261%	50%	£789	46%	33.3%
Hythe	£32	£49	22%	£88	79%	33.3%	£400	355%	50%	£583	50%	33.3%
New Romney		£39		£62	59%	33.3%	£247	298%	50%	£360	136%	33.3%
Ramsgate	£98	£174	79%*	£250	44%	100%	£1,452	101%	50%	£3,431	-22%	33.3%
Bromley		£97	*	£142	46%	100%	£503	135%	50%	£390	-48%	33.3%
Footscray				£421	44%	50%	£333	120%	50%	£173	102%	33.3%
Sevenoaks	£159	£292	84%†	£614	34%	33.3%	£926	165%	33.3%	£1,867	252%	50%
Tonbridge	£196	£457	133%				£1,211		33.3%	£1,854		40%
Tunbridge Wells	£63									£2,308		40%
Stonecrouch												
Lamberhurst	£47	£75	59%	£106	41%	33.3%	£851	91%	33.3%	£1,973	97%	40%
Cranbrook	£30	£87	190%	£122	40%	33.3%	£202	173%	33.3%	£622	208%	40%
Tenterden	£7						£333			£421	23%	60%
Biddenden							£25					
	£3,347	£8,264	140%	£9,536	17%		£29,641	211%		£43,652	47%	

FOOTNOTES

*Rate to London reduced from 3d. to 1d.   †Rate to London reduced from 3d. to 2d.

Figures for receipts given to the nearest £. Percentage increases given to the nearest whole number. Percentage increases in postage rates...

4. A rising population.[13]

5. The rise in seaside and resort traffic.[14]

These same factors ought to apply to the period following 1800, with the exception that military traffic would fall off dramatically after 1815.[15] Why, therefore, the much slower advance in revenue? This might be explained by the widespread evasion of postage especially following the rate increase of 1812' At the same time the relative profitability was adversely affected by:

1. The increase in the number of free items (newspapers and franked letters) that had to be carried.[16]

2. The need to provide free delivery within an increasing number of post towns and the extensions of free delivery boundaries at others.[17]

3. Until the end of the Napoleonic Wars the high cost of conveyance caused in large measure by the price of animal feed.[18]

New posts opened under fifth clause and penny post regulations,[19] were designed with the object of providing local services that would cover their own costs but add little to the General Post Revenue in most cases. Most of the factors listed would of course have affected postal revenue in all parts of Britain in this period.

Changes in Post Routes

Although the basic pattern, existing by 1784, of the two main post roads was not changed, many improvements were effected in routings and frequency of service. Details of these are shown in appendix seven.[20] They can be summarised as:

1. The increasing use of mail carts and coaches.

2. The establishment of cross post routes, the most important of which were the Hastings to Dover route opened in November 1827 and the Ashford to Canterbury route in August 1830. The Dartford to Sevenoaks fifth clause post also connected the Dover and Hastings Roads. Such cross posts enabled letters to reach their

LONDON

DARTFORD

FOOTSCRAY

GRAVESEND

ROCHESTER

Cl

BROMLEY

West Malling   3

SEVENOAKS

MAIDSTOI

TONBRIDGE

Goudhurst

TUNBRIDGE WELLS

Biddeno

LAMBERHURST

HAV

BATTLE

HASTII

Routes Operated all the Year by Coaches
Official Posts — 6 days a week
Official Posts — Less than 6 days
          (number of days operated indicated)
Sub Offices shown in lower case letters

KENTISH POST ROUTES 1790

QUEENBOROUGH

MARGATE

Ramsgate

RNE

FAVERSHAM

CANTERBURY   WINGHAM   SANDWICH

DEAL

ASHFORD

DOVER

FOLKESTONE
HYTHE   4

DEN

NEW ROMNEY

YE

destinations by a more direct route avoiding London, and as postage was charged strictly by the number of miles conveyed, this would show a saving both in time and postage.

3. The improved frequency of service. Many routes which in 1784 had only a three-day post, had by 1840 a daily post.

Appendix 7 does not show all the route additions effected as many of these were carried out under fifth clause and penny post regulations.[21] No mention is made either of the improved speed of transit especially by mail coaches, the result of better techniques in road construction and maintenance.[22]

Mail Conveyance

(a) Road Conditions

The introduction in 1784 of fast mail coaches and the increasing use of carts at the same period made the Post Office more concerned with road conditions. A road that was fit for a horse post was not necessarily fit for a mail coach. Although many Kentish roads had been turnpiked, their condition varied considerably. The Dover Road provided little or no trouble and must have been well maintained. William Cobbett, no lover of turnpikes, could think of nothing worse to say of the Faversham to Sittingbourne section that that it was dusty. The branch from Canterbury to Deal was reported in March 1793 by Admiral McBride to be 'bad' and six years later it was described as 'the worst out of Canterbury'. As the post rider covered the distance of 18 miles after dark with a number of 'stoppages' in three hours the road must have been of a moderate standard.[23]

The Hastings and Rye Roads were still bad, despite the efforts of the turnpike trustees. Suggestions that coaches should be tried on the Rye journey were rejected as impracticable in January 1793, and even the use of carts was found difficult. In December 1799 the contractors responsible for the conveyance of the mail to Hastings by cart complained of the state of the road, and Mr. Aust, the Post Office surveyor for the area, confirmed the contractor's complaints:

> the state of the Road from Woodsgate to Lamberhurst and from
> thence to Stonecrouch (except a small part which having been
> indicted, has been repaired) is such as not only to impede the
> progress of the mails but to be truly dangerous.

For this state of affairs he blamed the 'gross and culpable
neglect in the Parties whose business it was to attend to them
in the Seasons most proper for the purpose'.[24] When in 1801
renewal was sought by Act of Parliament for the powers of the
turnpike trustees for the Flimwell to Hastings turnpike, the
unsatisfactory state of the road was admitted. Clause VII of
the Act empowered the trustees to divert the road and build
a bridge at Robertsbridge. It was admitted that:

> Part of the said Road called *Robertsbridge Clappers* is from its low
> Situation subject and liable, to deep and dangerous Floods, inso-
> much that Passengers and Carriages are frequently stopped and
> delayed.[25]

By 1808 the road was still considered unsuitable for mail
coaches, and in July 1810 Mr. Scott, a Post Office surveyor,
was complaining that the

> London & Hastings Cart does not keep its time, the Contractors
> say the Road will not admit of it. The ride from Tunbridge to
> Maidstone is therefore frequently too late at the latter place for
> the dispatch to Ashford.

The poor state of the road was largely caused by the difficulty
in obtaining suitable repair materials. Giving evidence before
the Select Committee on the South-Eastern Railway Bill in
March 1836, Mr. William Knox Child, a local magistrate, landowner and trustee of the Sevenoaks to Woodsgate turnpike
declared 'we have no stones for 17 miles, we carry them from
Sevenoaks to Lamberhurst.[26]

Less important turnpikes and parish roads also varied considerably, depending upon their location and the amount of
maintenance. The problem of obtaining stone for road building
and repairing in the clay vales of the Weald was a constant
source of worry. A number of witnesses giving evidence in
favour of the South-Eastern Railway Bill of 1836 welcomed
the coming of the railway because it would bring road-repairing
materials to the area cheaply. William Hinds, a landowner and
turnpike trustee of Smarden, declared that the buying and
haulage of stone had placed the local trust from Benenden

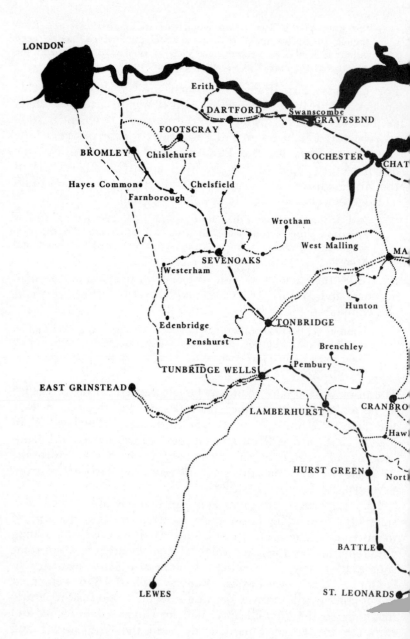

LONDON

Erith

DARTFORD

Swanscombe
GRAVESEND

FOOTSCRAY

ROCHESTER
CHAT

BROMLEY
Chislehurst

Hayes Common
Farnborough
Chelsfield

Wrotham

West Malling
MA

SEVENOAKS
Westerham

Hunton

Edenbridge
Penshurst

TONBRIDGE

Brenchley

TUNBRIDGE WELLS
Pembury

EAST GRINSTEAD

LAMBERHURST
CRANBRO

Haw

HURST GREEN
Nort

BATTLE

LEWES

ST. LEONARDS

KENTISH POST ROUTES 1839

SHEERNESS
Minster
Eastchurch
BOROUGH   Leysdown

Herne Bay
Whitstable   Sarre

MARGATE

Broadstairs

RAMSGATE

FAVERSHAM

WINGHAM   SANDWICH
Newnham   CANTERBURY   Ash
Selling

Godmersham   DEAL

                                                Walmer
Wye
                        Ewell
n
ASHFORD   Elham
        Bradbourne Lees
n   DOVER

FOLKESTONE
HYTHE
NTERDEN

Brookland
NEW ROMNEY

Lydd

— — —	Mail Coach Routes
·············	Other General Post Routes
·—·—·—·	Penny Post or Fifth Clause

to Charing in debt to the extent of £4,500, while no interest had been paid for 10 years. Of the 20 miles of minor roads in Smarden parish, he declared them to be so soft that farmers had no option but to join up their teams to one waggon and take half a load at a time. After winter frosts, such roads were impassable.[27]

The only action that the Post Office could take, if parish authorities or turnpike trustees failed to keep the roads in good condition, was to prosecute them before the local Justices of the Peace at the Quarter Sessions. In December 1799, Mr. Aust was able to report the section of the Hastings Road south of Lamberhurst as satisfactory, since the trustees had been indicted and had in consequence attended to the road during the summer months. He proposed to take similar action against the trustees for the section from Woodsgate to Lamberhurst at the Spring Assizes in Maidstone. This course of action was not always successful. Actions brought against three parishes on the Lamberhurst to Tenterden road earlier in the year 1799 were dismissed. Juries were inclined to sympathise with the parishes despite the unquestionable duty of the parish authorities to maintain the roads in good condition.[28]

(b) Mail Coaches

Following the successful introduction of mail coaches on the Bath Road in 1784, the route to Dover was quickly changed to this mode of conveyance, the first coach commencing to run on 31 October 1785. This service picked up passengers in London at the *George and Blue Boar,* Holborn, and the Gloucester Coffee House, Piccadilly, at 7.30 pm., before proceeding to the Post Office to load the mails for departure at 8 pm. The route followed was that of the post cart that the service replaced, passing through Dartford, Gravesend, Rochester, Sittingbourne, Faversham, and Canterbury. Two changes were, however, subsequently effected. From April 1821 the coach ran via Chatham, thus avoiding the need to convey the mail from Rochester at midnight. In April 1834 Faversham was by-passed, and a foot messenger was appointed to meet the coach and take the mails into the town from the main road.[29]

Apart from the daily Dover coach with the inland mails for north and east Kent, there was also a special coach to convey the foreign mails. Its departure from London varied to some extent with the state of the tide at Dover, which influenced the sailing time of the packets. Up to 10 November 1792 the foreign mails had to be conveyed to Dover twice a week by cart under contracts made with the postmasters of Southwark, Dartford, Rochester, Sittingbourne, and Canterbury. By July 1792, however, the Post Office were making arrangements for conveyance by coach. The cancellation of the contracts for carriage by cart must have been very sudden, for the Post Office felt obliged to continue payments to the contractors up to the end of the quarter as compensation.[30]

The life of the coach was initially short. The declaration of war on France in February 1793 closed the Calais to Dover route, and the rapid advance of the armed forces of the Republic into the Low Countries made the crossing to Flanders dangerous and invonvenient. At the outbreak of the war a London to Harwich coach was established to convey the bulk of the continental mail via Holland. The small number of passengers wanting to travel over the Dover route to the continent obliged the contractors to apply in July 1794 to Thomas Hasker, the Post Office Mail Coach Superintendent, for the cancellation of the contract. Hasker persuaded them to continue as the military operations constituted but 'a temporary check to travelling that road'.[31] In October he was obliged to agree to the re-timing of the coach to depart at the more convenient time of 5 pm. from London in the hope that more passenger traffic might be attracted.[32] The discontinuation of the packets between Dover and Flushing a few months later finally put an end to the service until the cessation of hostilities.

Mail coaches between Canterbury and Margate must have been established soon after those to Dover. On 29 June 1793 Thomas Hasker sought permission to commence the service from 8 July for a season of 20 weeks, by the same contractor and on the same terms as the previous year. The wording of the request implied that the coach had been operating for at least a year previously. Requests made in 1795 for a similar coach from Canterbury to Ramsgate during the season were refused. The only results of the petitions were that Ramsgate was made a post town, and the mail by way of Sandwich was speeded up. Agreement was however reached for a coach for the 1807 season. Both coaches were still operating in 1834, though because of their seasonal nature they were not always listed on the maps of mail coach routes. During the remainder of the year horse posts served the two towns.[33]

Permission to establish the Canterbury to Deal coach was given in September 1792, but the service was probably never started. Nothing more is heard of coaches on this route until March 1823 when a regular service was commenced, which from the mid-1830s was operated by a pair horse coach. A further mail coach route from Dover to New Romney was established in July 1822 but was discontinued after a year and replaced by a mail cart.[34]

Mail coaches were slow to appear on the Hastings Road. A proposal was made as early as May 1793 for a coach to replace the Rye cart. Nothing came of this. The idea was renewed in November 1805, but it was not until 5 June 1811 that a service by coach was started. Cary's map of mail coach routes issued in 1811 shows the route, but it is missing from the 1812 and subsequent editions. Certainly by November 1813 the Hastings mail had reverted to being carried by mail cart. No further attempt was made to set up mail coaches to Hastings until 1821 from which date the coach became permanent. In 1836 the coach route was extended to St. Leonards. One other coach on this road carried mail. This was the stage coach which for a time carried bags from Bromley to Farnborough. This route is shown on a map dated 28 February 1813, and the coach was still in use in January 1817, but exact dates for the commencement and cessation of the service cannot be determined.[35]

The Dover Inland Mail Coach was one of the patent mail coaches supplied on hire by the Millbank coachworks under contract. This coachworks was controlled up to his death in 1791 by a man called John Bessant, and until the contract expired in 1836 by his partner John Vidler and his children.[36] The coaches carried four inside passengers and initially one outside, later increased to three or four. Horses and coachmen were provided under contract, and the contractor was the beneficiary of the passenger fares. The guard was provided by the Post Office. The London to Dover Inland Mail Coach, however, was the only four-horse vehicle of this type in Kent, the remaining coaches being ordinary stage vehicles. They usually carried four outside passengers, but sometimes as many as eight. Most of the coaches were hauled by four horses, the Dover Foreign Mail and the Canterbury to Margate coaches being of this type. Other coaches such as the London to Hastings and the Canterbury to Deal were only drawn by two horses.[37]

When John Palmer inaugurated mail coach transit, the time of departure from the General Post Office in London of all mail coaches was set at 8 pm. A timebill of 1797 lists the time of arrival at Dover as 6.30 am., with a 20-minute break at Canterbury to sort letters. This gives an average speed, including stops, for the 74 miles of just over seven miles per hour. This was appreciably better than that achieved by the post riders that the coach had replaced. The return journey left Dover at 6.30 pm., reaching London at 5.20 am., with a similar delay at Canterbury. This timing appears to have satisfied the Post Office and was not improved upon until the 1830s.[38] In 1836 the Dover Inland Mail departing from London at 8 pm. was reaching Dover at 4.57 am., an average speed of 8.2 miles per hour. This much-improved timing enabled the departure of the return coach from Dover to be put back to 9.45 am., a more convenient time for travelling. By 1838 the speed had been improved further, and 10 miles 3 furlongs per hour was recorded as the official speed of the coach. The Dover Foreign Mail, though not a patent coach, and more heavily loaded with passengers, was also a fast vehicle. In 1837 it was the fastest coach on the road, despite the fact that much of the journey took place at night. The coach left London at 12 midnight and arrived at Dover at 8.15 am. at an average speed of nearly nine miles an hour. The coach departed again for London at 10 am.[39]

The speed of the connecting coach to Margate tended to be rather slower. In 1797 it departed from Canterbury 25 minutes after the Dover Inland Mail from London, i.e., at 4.50 am. The coach arrived at Margate at 7.15 am., having taken 2 hours 25 minutes to cover the 17 miles, an average of just over seven miles an hour. The return journey to Canterbury started at 5 pm. and arrived at 7.45 pm., giving a slower average speed of 6.2 m.p.h. The easier timing may have been deliberate to ensure the connection with the London mail coach was not missed. By 1834 the timings had been improved. The departure time of both the Margate and Ramsgate coaches was 8.30 pm., and Canterbury was reached at 10.40 pm., an average speed of 7.8 miles per hour. The Deal to Canterbury coach using only a pair of horses was slower, averaging only six miles an hour in 1838. It was reported to be the slowest coach in the country conveying mail. On the Hastings Road, also using two horses, the coach was scheduled to reach Hastings at 5.14 am., covering the 67 miles from London in 9 hours 14 minutes, at an average speed of just over 7.2 miles per hour. On the return journey the coach left Hastings at 9 am. In 1797 when the mail was being conveyed by cart, it took over 12 hours to complete the journey, including no less than an hour and 10 minutes delay for the sorting of letters at Lamberhurst and Battle.[40]

The main contractor for the mail coaches on the Dover Road at their commencement was Christopher Ibbertson, whose London headquarters was the *George and Blue Boar* in Holborn. For the Dover Inland Mail he provided the horses as far as Canterbury, where William Miles took over. Ibbertson was also involved with Miles and Thomas Rutley as contractors for the Dover Foreign Mail. The name of the contractor for the Canterbury to Margate coach at this period was Benson. By 1814 a new contractor was involved in the Dover Inland Mail. This was John Eames whose coaching inn was *The Angel*, St. Clements in the Strand. Eames was also contractor for the Portsmouth and Gloucester Mails and ran stage coaches on his own account to Salisbury, Portsmouth, Cheltenham, Farringdon, Wantage, Henley, Bath and Godalming.[41] By the 1830s the contractor for the Dover Inland Mail was Benjamin Worthy Horne who worked in conjunction with William Chaplin whose coaching inn, *The Swan with Two Necks* in Lad Lane, was located near the new General Post Office in St Martins-le-Grand. Chaplin was one of the largest coach proprietors in the kingdom and controlled 1,800 horses and 106 coaches. The Dover Foreign Mail and the Hastings Mail were contracted to William Horne of the *Golden Cross*, Charing Cross and the *Cross Keys*, Wood Street. When he died in 1828, the business was carried on by his son, Benjamin Worthy Horne, who was also contractor for the mail coaches to Gloucester, Chester and Stroud. The Hastings Mail started from the *Bolt-in-Tun,* Fleet Street, calling also at the *Golden Cross,* Charing Cross.[42]

Giving evidence before a parliamentary committee in December 1827, Mr. C. Johnson, the Mail Coach Superintendent for the Post Office, stated that the usual payment to coach proprietors was 3d. per double mile, but admitted that there were many exceptions. The Dover Inland Mail appears to have been paid at 2d. a double mile in 1790, rising to 4d. in 1800, and falling again to 3d. in 1805. At this rate it continued until 1835.[43] In 1838 the conveyance of letters by the Dover Inland Mail was costing £452 16s. 6d. or four and one-eighth pence per double mile. The Dover Foreign Mail was an exception to the usual method of payment, for it was not contracted for on a mileage basis. A sum of £600 was paid to the contractors yearly, but they were obliged to provide carts to convey the mail to London if the packets arrived at Dover after the mail coach had departed. Rates for two horse coaches were usually lower. In 1838 the Deal coach from Canterbury was costing 3d. a double mile, but that to Hastings from London cost only 2¼d. a double mile. Where mail was conveyed in a stage coach under contract, rates could be lower still. In 1817 the contractor conveying the mail from Bromley to Farnborough by coach was paid only £5 a year, while in the case of the Canterbury to Margate Coach only 2d. a double mile was allowed. This was substantially below the cost of conveyance by mail cart or rider. Operating mail coaches bestowed one great advantage on the contractors; that was freedom from tolls. John Eames, contractor for the Dover Inland Mail, admitted that in his case freedom from tolls on this one coach was worth £6 10s. 0d. a week. This gave a useful advantage to mail coaches, especially the contractors using non-patent vehicles who were not obliged to conform to Post Office regulations regarding the number of passengers.[44]

Kent was well served by coaches. A newspaper advertisement for the *Golden Cross* Coach Office in January 1806 listed coaches for Tunbridge Wells (two departures), Hastings, Maidstone, Folkestone, Dover, Margate, Ramsgate, Deal, and Gravesend (four departures). The *Cross Keys* Coach Office offered in addition two daily departures for Dover, Deal, Ramsgate,

Margate and Canterbury.[45] Evidence given by Mr. John Swainson, Clerk of the Stage Coach Duty Office in March 1836, showed the considerable number of coaches then on the Kentish roads:

No. of coaches	From	To	No. of journeys each week
1	London	Sevenoaks	12
1	,,	Sundridge	12
1	,,	Westerham	2
5	,,	Tunbridge Wells	42
8	,,	Maidstone	82
13	,,	Canterbury	91
2	,,	Folkestone	12
13	,,	Dover	94
2	,,	Rye	12
10	,,	Hastings	69
4	Canterbury	Deal	54
7	,,	Dover	70[46]

All these stage coaches competed with the mail coaches for passengers, and it was passenger fares that subsidised the carriage of mail. Each stage coach was a potential carrier of letters which should legally have passed through the Post Office. In their turn the coaches, both stage and mail, had to face competition from steamships service the north coast of the county and Thanet. In 1811 the fare by mail coach from London to Dover was £2 inside or £1 2s. 0d. outside. By the 1830s it was possible by using steam vessels to reach Herne Bay in six hours, taking another four hours to reach Dover by road. The total cost could be as low as 10s. 0d. These boats were also capable of conveying letters illegally. In 1838 it was taking the Post Office 10 hours to carry letters from London to Margate. A steamship could perform the same journey in seven hours.[47]

(c) Mail Carts and Horse Posts

During the period 1784 to 1824 mail coaches took over from mail carts on several Kentish routes, but they were retained for those routes where the need for a passenger service was small or the journey was commenced at an hour of the day inconvenient for passengers. Mail carts were supplied and maintained by the contractors and were probably not uniform in appearance. On important routes like that from London to Hastings, before the mail coach was established, covered carts were hauled by two horses. A guard also travelled with this particular cart. Most carts must have been two-wheeled, though one contractor on the Hastings Road was in 1821 using a four-wheeled one. The vehicles did have to provide adequate security for the mail conveyed, and the contractor for the Canterbury to Margate route was dismissed in April 1835 for conveying the mail 'in a common Tax Cart with a chest placed upon it' to contain the mail bags.[48] The routes still using mail carts in January 1824 are shown in Table VII. From 1824 to 1840 the number of routes where conveyance was by means of mail carts increased. This was caused partly by the establishment of new routes like that from Ashford to Canterbury, and partly by the discontinuance of certain mail coaches in East Kent. In addition to those shown as operating in 1824, the following new routes had come into being by 1838:

> Canterbury to Ashford
> Canterbury to Herne Bay
> Canterbury to Margate and Ramsgate
> Dover to Deal
> Maidstone to Cranbrook
> New Romney to Hastings.

Some routes before the 1820s, and a few minor ones after this period, were still operated by horse riders. It is not possible, with a few exceptions, to distinguish them, as documents of this period refer to 'Riding work' whether carts were used or not, and official maps mark the routes as 'horse posts'. As the amount of mail increased so the need for a cart became more pressing. Even some penny post routes were using carts by 1840. A return of 1838 failed to mention any route where

TABLE VI

List of the Main Kentish Routes Operated by Mail Cart—January 1824

Route				Distance	Time of Departure	Time of Arrival	Time taken	Speed m.p.h.
Maidstone to Ashford	..	..	..	20 miles	4.50 am.	8 am.	3hrs. 10min.	6.3 m.p.h.
Ashford to Maidstone	..	..	..	20 ,,	5.15 pm.	8.40 pm.	3hrs. 25min.	5.6 m.p.h.
Maidstone to Tonbridge	..	..	..	14 ,,	9.15 pm.	11.35 pm.	2hrs. 20min.	6 m.p.h.
Tonbridge to Maidstone	..	..	..	14 ,,	1.50 am.	4 am.	2hrs. 10min.	6.5 m.p.h.
Rochester to Maidstone	..	..	..	9 ,,	2 am.	3.30 am.	1hr. 30min.	6 m.p.h.
Maidstone to Rochester	..	..	..	9 ,,	10 pm.	11.15 pm.	1hr. 15min.	7.2 m.p.h.
Dover to New Romsey	..	..	..	20 ,,	6.30 pm.	9.50 pm.	3hrs. 20 min.	6 m.p.h.
New Romsey to Dover	..	..	..	20 ,,	4 pm.	7.20 pm.	3hrs. 20min.	6 m.p.h.

Sources: P.O.R. Post 40/275/65; Post 42/110/352.

the mail was carried by 'saddle horse' for the whole of Kent, all routes, except those of mail coaches, being listed as 'mail carts' or 'foot posts', though it is possible that some minor routes were served by horsed messengers.[49]

Riding work was carried out under contract, for which the usual period appears to have been a year. During the 17th century the postmasters had contracted for riding work, which had been considered almost as part of their duty, and at the end of the 18th century there were still postmasters undertaking such work. Particularly on longer routes, however, the work was being put out to general contract. With the increase in coaching, horse hire was no doubt concentrated in fewer hands, those who had the resources to take on large contracts. People who were appointed postmasters were no longer innkeepers or interested in horse hire. It was the responsibility of the Post Office Surveyor for the region to negotiate contracts. After advertisements had been inserted in the local newspapers, inviting tenders, the surveyor checked the ability of those tendering to carry out the contract. A newspaper advertisement in 1831 for the Canterbury to Ashford ride produced seven tenders ranging from £125 to £165 per ammum. The lowest tender was not accepted as it was submitted by someone who in the opinion of the surveyor was not a 'fit person'.[50]

From the middle of the 18th century until the outbreak of the Napoleonic Wars, the accepted rate for riding work was £4 3s. 4d. per double mile per year. On routes where mail was conveyed less than six days a week a lesser sum was given. This settled basis of payment had to be abandoned as the prices of animal feed rose with the onset of the Napoleonic conflict. Early in 1799, Mr. Hanson, the Sevenoaks postmaster, responsible for the riding work from Sevenoaks to Lamberhurst, petitioned to be freed from his contract on which he was losing money. In November 1799 the contractor for the Canterbury to Deal road petitioned for an increased allowance, and temporary increases had to be granted to mail coach contractors.[51] In this year prices of animal feed rose to new heights, and by July 1800 oats in the Canterbury market were fetching around 49s. a quarter, about two and a third times the pre-war price levels.[52] Although prices had fallen by September 1804, the

Post Office Surveyor for the region endorsed claims for increased allowances by declaring that:

> the Prices of Horse Provender in Kent and Sussex are very greatly advanced by the consumption of the great number of cavalry there.

The violent upsurge of feed prices in 1812–3 resulted in a further spate of requests for increased allowances. Additions had to be made if the service was to be continued efficiently. The contractors for the Dover to New Romney ride were paid an extra £30 per annum in March 1813 'during the high prices of provender'. The Post Office was also obliged to apply for Treasury consent to pay additional allowances to mail coach contractors in January 1813.[53] One route which showed the rising cost of conveyance well was that from London to Hastings and Rye. Figures for that road are given in Appendix 4, pp. 147-9.

Contractors were forbidden to carry either parcels or passengers on mail carts, because it might result in delay and place the mails at risk. In November 1808 the Post Office received complaints from the Stamp Office that the Dover to New Romney, and Canterbury to Thanet mail carts were conveying passengers illegally, as they were unlicenced vehicles. The area Post Office Surveyor, Mr. Aust, reported that the Sandwich to Margate contractor kept better time in winter than in summer, and this he felt could 'only be attributed to his carrying heavier loads and paying more attention to his passengers than to the service'. The result was the dismissal of the existing contractors and negotiations for new contracts, which were entered into at a considerably higher rate. In support of the increased cost Francis Freeling, the Secretary to the Post Office, wrote to the Postmasters-General:

> That your Lordships may be fully satisfied of the reasons of this expense I beg to remark that to permit any extraneous cause such as carriage of Passengers and Luggage to operate against the Dispatch of important mails, it is at all times improper.

The conveyance of parcels was practiced by some contractors including the one who conveyed the London to Hastings mails up to his dismissal in May 1821. He conveyed 'fish and parcels of every description in his Mail Cart'. Even if the contractor did not break the terms of his contract, his employee was liable

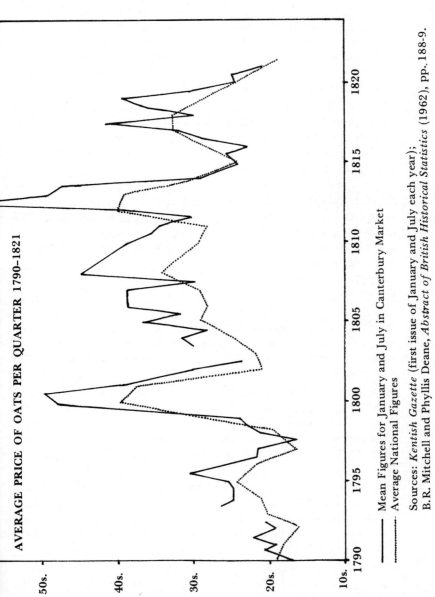

AVERAGE PRICE OF OATS PER QUARTER 1790–1821

Mean Figures for January and July in Canterbury Market
Average National Figures

Sources: *Kentish Gazette* (first issue of January and July each year);
B.R. Mitchell and Phyllis Deane, *Abstract of British Historical Statistics* (1962), pp. 188-9.

to do so. Messrs. Boorman and Huggett, when first negotiating for the London to Lamberhurst contract in June 1806, asked for the wages of the guards on the carts to be raised to £1 a week. The new contractors were convinced that Mr. Tibbs, the previous contractor, had lost money on the contract because his men were carrying 'heavy luggage' on the carts. This was damaging the carts and placing a strain on the horses. The new contractors were determined to stop this illegal carriage of goods but realised that 'the men's Emoluments' were 'very much lessened by this being put a stop to'.[54]

With the improved speed and frequency of delivery of the mails the need for expresses declined. They appear to have continued in use intermittently for three purposes. One was the conveyance of mails that arrived late by packet after the regular means of conveyance had left, or for mails that had been landed at ports other than their usual destination. The contract for the Dover Foreign Mail Coach made provision for the the transport of mails arriving late, but before 1792 when this coach was established, the use of expresses when the packets were late appears to have been common. Adverse sailing conditions at times obliged the packets to sail to Margate and if the post had already left, expresses had to be provided. In March 1794, the Margate postmaster claimed for three such expresses to Canterbury. The use of expresses was more frequent in the period following 1828 when briefly the station for the Ostend packets was established at Margate.[55] The resoration of these packets to Dover combined with a later departure of the mail coach from April 1830 reduced the number of expresses. The second user of expresses were military establishments, especially the dockyard and garrison at Sheerness. In March 1793 it was agreed to pay the ferry keeper at The King's Ferry 40s. a year salary and a shilling for each express to ensure that they were forwarded rapidly. It was stated that there had only been four expresses the whole of the previous year, but under war conditions it was likely that there would be more. Thirdly, it was necessary at times to forward letters express intended for persons of importance in government. William Pitt, Lord Liverpool and the Duke of Wellington were all resident at certain periods at Walmer Castle. Provision was made for the letters to be despatched to them from Deal in a special pouch, but an express would be needed if, as in September 1829, the letter (in this case for the Duke of Wellington) was wrongly despatched to Dover. Figures for the amounts paid to postmasters for government expresses exist for the years 1800 and 1835:

TABLE VIII

Amounts Paid to Kentish Postmasters for the Conveyance of Government Expresses

Office				1800			1835		
				£	s.	d.	£	s.	d.
Canterbury ..	..	..	17	11	6	—		
Dartford	..	..	..	33	14	4	2	5	10
Deal ..	..	..	..	2	2	9		14	8
Dover	..	..	..	5	6	6	—		
Gravesend	..	..	..		6	6	—		
Rochester	..	..	..	21	6	0	—		
Sittingbourne	..	..	16	4	3	1	19	5	
Sheerness	..	..	..	1	12	0	—		
Bromley	..	..	..	4	2	9		19	3
Sevenoaks	..	..	..	4	4	7	—		
			£106	11	2	£5	19	2	

Sources: P.O.R. Post 3/20, 3/21, 3/24, 3/25.

It was possible for private persons to send letters express. but the cost of transit was high and the service little used. In May 1826 the rates were 11d. a mile with a fee of 2s. 6d. allowed to the postmasters. Private expresses other than to London were discouraged.[56]

(d) Foot Posts

   A number of short routes continued to be operated by foot posts. Such arrangements were useful for connecting points on the routes of mail coaches with post towns situated a short distance from the route. An example is Tunbridge Wells, where in June 1827 the mail coach ceased serving the town and was routed on the direct road to Hastings. A foot post was estab- lished to convey the mail from Tonbridge to Tunbridge Wells.

TABLE IX

List of Kentish Foot Posts—January 1824

Route				Distance	Time of Departure	Time of Arrival	Time Taken	Speed m.p.h.
Hawkhurst to Biddenden	..	..	..	10 miles	5.45 am.	7.45 am.	2hrs.	5 m.p.h.
Biddenden to Hawkhurst	..	..	..	10 ,,	3.30 pm.	7.35 pm.	4hrs. 5min.	2.5 m.p.h.
Newenden to Tenterden	..	..	..	6 ,,	5.30 am.	7.10 am.	1hr. 40min.	3.6 m.p.h.
Tenterden to Newenden	..	..	..	6 ,,	5.30 pm.	7.30 pm.	2hrs.	3 m.p.h.
Ramsgate to Margate	..	..	..	6 ,,	7.45 am.	9 am.	1hr. 15min.	4 m.p.h.
Margate to Ramsgate	..	..	..	6 ,,	4.50 pm.	6 pm.	1hr. 30min.	3 m.p.h.
Sittingbourne to Sheerness	..	..	..	12 ,,	4.30 am.	7.30 am.	3hrs.	4 m.p.h.
Sheerness to Sittingbourne	..	..	..	12 ,,	6.15 pm.	9.45 pm.	3hrs. 30min.	3.4 m.p.h.
Tonbridge to Tunbridge Wells	..	..	..	6 ,,	5 am.	7 am.	2hrs.	3 m.p.h.
Tunbridge Wells to Tonbridge	..	..	..	6 ,,	8.30 pm.	10.30 pm.	2hrs.	3 m.p.h.

Sources: P.O.R. Post 40/275/65; Post 43/110/352.

Foot posts were restricted in the distance that they could travel. Reductions were made in 1827 to the length of the journey of the Sevenoaks to Kemsing and Wrotham messenger who travelled 26 miles a day, and the Dartford to Kemsing messenger whose route was 28 miles, because the duty was considered excessive. Thus when routes were extended in distance a change from foot to horse posts might be necessary. This occurred in July 1835 when the Maidstone to Staplehurst route was extended to Cranbrook. A change from foot to horse post would also be necessary if the weight of mail increased beyond the capacity of the foot post to cope. The speed of the foot post was naturally slow. In January 1824, a return showed the speed of the Kentish footposts as between 2½ and 5 miles per hour.

One important route that continued to be operated by a foot post was that from Sittingbourne to Sheerness, for a foot post could take a path through the marshes close to the estuary, a much more direct route than was possible by a horse. The great advantage of the foot post was its cheapness. In January 1811 the ride from Hawkhurst to Tenterden was replaced by two foot posts, one from Hawkhurst to Biddenden and the other from Newenden to Tenterden. The result was a reduction in cost from £108 2s. 6d. to £77 10s. 0d. p.a.[57]

From the point of view of cost of conveyance, the mail cart was the most expensive. In 1829 the cost of conveying the mails by this means for the country as a whole averaged £8 6s. 1½d. per double mile per annum. Where the load was less and the cart unnecessary the cost of a horse post averaged £7 3s. 7d. per double mile. Mail coaches, subsidised by the passengers conveyed, averaged only £5 19s. 3½d. per double mile, while the foot messengers were the least expensive at an average of £4 9s. 8½d. On the Kentish routes in 1838 the cheapeast mail cart contracts were those from Dover to New Romney and Maidstone to Cranbrook, both paid at £8 per double mile; the most expensive that between Canterbury and Ramsgate and Margate paid at £11 per double mile. The average for the 11 Kentish rides was £9 1s. 3d. per double mile. Of the 17 foot posts the lowest paid was the Faversham to Boughton at £2 12s. 0d. per double mile, and the highest Gravesend to Northfleet at £13 per double mile, though this post made two deliveries a day. The average rate was £5 8s. 9d. per double mile. [58]

Military Mail

One factor that stands out clearly from Table V[59] is the way in which in 1800 military installations within the county were inflating the postal traffic of certain post towns, particularly Sheerness, Deal, Folkestone, and Hythe. In the case of Sheerness and Deal the sequel is shown in the much lower figures for 1835 which are substantially down despite an increase in postage rates. The Hythe and Folkestone receipts continued to increase between 1800 and 1835, probably an indication of a rise in summer visitors and greater residential development on the coast.[60] Camps were set up for troops at Barham Down, near Canterbury, Brabourne Leas, near Ashford, and at Shorncliffe and Lydd. All the camps had to be provided with connections to the existing postal system to ensure that the military authorities received their mail promptly. To serve the Shorncliffe Camp an application was made in June 1794 for a new post from Canterbury to Folkestone, but this was refused on the grounds of cost and the mail continued to be routed by way of Dover, but the speed accelerated. An orderly collected the mail from Folkestone. The extra duties involved by the need to deal with this traffic had to be paid for, and in July 1794 the receivers at Sandgate and Lydd had their annual salaries increased by two guineas, and those of the postmasters at Folkestone, Hythe, and New Romney were reviewed. The camp at Barham Down was served by the Dover mail coach, and the postmaster at Canterbury awarded an extra guinea a week in July 1795 for sorting the camp letters. A military allowance of £20 per annum was still being paid in April 1817 as the barracks were still 'full of troops'. Between Ashford and Brabourne Lees a special military post was set up which, when it was replaced in December 1816 by a penny post, was costing a guinea a week to maintain apart from the additional allowance of £18 4s. 0d. per annum for the Ashford postmaster. In July 1793 a camp was set up near Tunbridge Wells, but in August the troops moved off to Brighton. The Tunbridge Wells postmaster was paid 5s. a day extra for sorting the letters.[61]

The landings of the British forces on the Dutch coast in 1799 and 1809 provided headaches for the Kentish postmasters involved in distributing mail to the troops. Many of the soldiers involved in the Helder Campaign of 1799 had been stationed at Barham Down. Their place was taken by militia units. This movement of troops caused trouble enough for the postmaster of Canterbury, but this must have increased further in November when British troops were evacuated. On 25 November he was complaining of the large number of letters that had come back from Holland and 'are continually travelling from one town to another after their respective regiments—our Cross Road Bags are consequently very heavy'. The 1809 Walcheren Expedition brought similar trouble. The forces were served by a packet route from Harwich to Flushing, but at the end of August 1809 the Deal postmaster claimed that he had 20,000 letters for men in the expedition, and arrangements were made for a special coach to convey the letters to London from Canterbury. In May 1810 the Ramsgate postmaster asked for some remuneration for his fatigue and trouble concerned with troop embarkations from the port in the last three years. He wrote:

> the constant change of Troops, the change of Lodgings of the Officers, the Letters to be left till called for, the Transport Service &c &c demand all my energies and thank God they were such as I trust left no one to find fault with my conduct.

He was granted £20 for his expenses and £20 for his extra work[62]

Mail for the naval base at Sheerness provided problems of a special nature because of the ferry to the Isle of Sheppey. To ensure continuity of service, the ferryman was given protection against impressment and offered £5 per annum. Despite this, complaints about lateness continued, especially in times of bad weather. In March 1795, the Lieutenant Governor of Sheerness suggested to the Post Office that they construct a sliding bridge to replace the ferry. He was informed that the Post Office had no authority to build bridges, and that if one was needed it should be provided by the Navy Board, the Treasury, or the Admiralty.[63] At the outbreak of hostilities in 1793 there was no post office at Sheerness and letters were collected from the Queenborough post office by a servant

TABLE X

Returned Letters from Kentish Offices—Year Ending 5 January 1801

Office	Total value of letters received	Total value of letters returned	Percentage
	£	£	%
Ashford	670	77	11.5
Canterbury	2,975	211	7.5
Chatham	2,267	227	10
Dartford..	776	65	8.3
Deal	2,398	480	20
Dover	2,067	183	8.9
Faversham	821	38	4.6
Folkestone	542	33	6.1
Gravesend	1,000	87	8.7
Hythe	400	33	6.1
Maidstone	2,424	115	4.7
Margate	1,553	59	3.8
New Romney	247	23	9.3
Queenborough..	214	16	7.5
Ramsgate	1,452	53	3.7
Rochester	1,824	178	9.8
Sandwich	527	20	3.8
Sittingbourne	504	18	3.6
Wingham	149	2	1.3
Sheerness	2,627	510	19.4
Bromley..	503	22	4.4
Cranbrook	202	6	3
Footscray	333	11	3.3
Lamberhurst	851	37	4.3
Sevenoaks	926	39	4.2
Tenterden	333	24	7.2
Tonbridge	1,211	56	4.7

Sources: P.O.R. Post 3/18, 3/19

appointed by the Commissioners of the Dockyard, who received a salary from the naval authorities and a gratuity of a penny on all letters delivered or received. In May 1799 Sheerness became a separate post town. Sheerness handled all the mail for the ships at the Nore. The stress of war made early delivery essential, and from January 1811 the mail left Sittingbourne at 3 am. enabling it to reach Sheerness by 7.30 am.[64]

One of the difficulties experienced by postmasters at naval stations was the delivery of letters sent to seamen. The post-master of Queenborough in September 1793 was of the opinion that only one letter in five addressed to seamen was ever delivered.

> the ships' boat comes on shore for Letters but the Officer of such boats, frequently a midshipman, does not know one third of the Ship's Company by name and if he did he has no money to take up the Letters, neither would he if he had, because he knows the Seamen have no Money to pay him again, he therefore takes only the Officer's Letters, the Seamen's lye in the office untill the Ship sails to another port, we then return the letters to the G.P. Office to forward after the Ships, but whether it is to the Downs, Ports-mouth or Plymouth the case is the same also there.

Certainly both Deal and Sheerness had a much greater number of returned letters than other Kentish offices. The figures for returned letters are given in Table X.[65]

Mail from Seaside and Inland Spas

There was a pronounced rise in the mail from resort towns, the most important of which were Margate and Ramsgate, and the Post Office recognised the value of this additional postal traffic. Special provision was made by using a mail coach to Ramsgate and Margate in the season, and the appointment of additional letter carriers in the summer months to deliver the increased mail. At Ramsgate in 1796 the mail amounted to £6 to £9 a week in the season, but fell to 20s. to 30s. weekly at other times. In 1812 it was stated that letters in the London bag from Margate in the winter did not average more than £3 9s. 0d., but in the summer they were three to four times that amount.[66] Smaller settlements that received a seasonal influx of visitors were also considered, and as early as July 1792 the Margate to Sandwich post route was altered to serve Broadstairs 'for the accommodation of the neighbourhood and company resorting thither'. A report dated January 1822 stated that 'during the Summer Months many Families are in the habit of resorting to Walmer for the purpose of bathing'. As a result a penny post route was set up from Deal to Walmer.[67]

Tunbridge Wells, in the mid-18th century averaged at least three times as many letters during the season as at other times of the year. It may have been more, as the accounts of the Tunbridge Wells and Tonbridge offices were included together. By the end of the century, however, the seasonal peak was becoming less pronounced, and the seaside resorts were attracting away those who had in the past flocked to inland spas. By 1835 mail delivered at Tunbridge Wells in the season was only a third higher than in the other months, both a reflection of the decline in summer visitors, and the rise in permanent inhabitants with such developments as the Calverley Estate. The combined populations of Tonbridge and Tunbridge Wells at the time of the 1801 census was 4,371; by 1841 it had risen to 12,530. The population of the coastal resorts was rising at a less spectacular rate, with the exception of Margate which was a town with a considerable residential population by the early 19th century.[68]

Population and Postal Revenue

Throughout the 18th and early 19th centuries the population of Kent was rising. For the first half of the 18th century the increase was moderate, a mere 0.17 per cent. per annum, but in the second half of the century this jumped dramatically to 1.66 per cent. per annum. The greatest rise occurred in the decade 1800–10, when the annual rise was just under 2 per cent. per annum. This had fallen off to 1.22 per cent. in the 1820s, but rose again to 1.51 per cent. in the next decade. From 1781 to 1811 the Kentish population was rising faster than that of England and Wales as a whole.[69]

With such a population rise, an increase in postal revenue of fairly substantial proportions ought to have resulted, regardless of such other factors, such as rising literacy and increasing

TABLE XI

Increase in Mail at Kentish Resorts in the Summer Months

	Average monthly value of letters received		% increase of summer months over a month in the rest of the year
	Oct.–June	July–Sept.	
1750	£ s. d.	£ s. d.	%
Dover	20 12 8	22 3 8	8.1
Folkestone	2 15 8	3 3 4	12.5
Margate (including Sandwich)	22 9 9	27 2 2	20-9
Ramsgate	Not a post town at this date		
Tunbridge Wells (including Tonbridge)	11 3 3	31 14 3	187.9
1800			
Dover	161 2 3	205 12 7	28
Folkestone	42 12 6	52 17 3	25
Margate	83 12 0	266 19 7	220
Ramsgate	84 3 10	231 6 11	175
Tunbridge Wells (including Tonbridge)	81 2 8	160 8 6	97.5
1835			
Dover	284 11 9	384 13 3	22.5
Folkestone	61 4 0	79 11 0	30.1
Margate	140 18 2	300 17 8	113.4
Ramsgate	250 14 0	391 10 7	54.9
Tunbridge Wells	184 12 3	248 19 4	35.6
Tonbridge	151 9 9	163 16 6	8.2

Sources: P.O.R. Post 3/12, 3/18, 3/19, 3/24, 3/25.

TABLE XII

Population Increase in Kentish Resort Towns

Town	1801	1811	1821	1831	1841	Percentage rise in population 1801–41	Percentage rise in postal revenue 1800–35
Dover	7,184	8,804	10,327	11,922	13,872	93.1%	75%
Folkestone	3,704	4,232	4,451	4,296	4,413	19.2%	46%
Margate	4,766	6,126	7,843	10,339	11,050	131.8%	40%
Ramsgate	3,100	4,221	6,031	7,985	10,909	218%	136%
Tunbridge Wells (including Tonbridge	4,371	5,932	7,406	10,380	12,530	186.6%	252%
County Population ..	308,667	368,350	426,016	478,028	548,177	77.6%	41.8%

Note.: Census dates are outside the usual resort season, e.g., 1801-10 March; 1811–27 May; 1821–28 May; 1831–20 May; 1841–7 June.

Sources: *V.C.H. Kent* (1932), Vol. 3, pp. 358ff.

Table V, pp. 101–3.

TABLE XIII

Population Rise in Kent, 1700–1841

Year	Population of England and Wales	Population of Kent	Percentage of Population of England and Wales	Increase in Population of Kent	Percentage increase	Percentage increase per annum
1701	5,826,000	155,694	2.7%			
1751	6,140,000	168,679	2.7%	12,985	8.3%	0.17%
1781	7,531,000	232,973	3.1%	64,294	38.1%	1.27%
1801	8,893,000	308,667	3.5%	75,694	32.5%	1.63%
1811	10,164,000	368,350	3.6%	59,683	19.3%	1.93%
1821	12,000,000	426,016	3.6%	57,766	15.7%	1.57%
1831	13,897,000	478,028	3.5%	52,012	12.2%	1.22%
1841	15,914,000	548,177	3.5%	70,149	15.1%	1.51%

Sources: Phyllis Deane and W. A. Cole, *British Economic Growth 1688–1959* (2nd edn, 1967), p. 103; B. R. Mitchell and Phyllis Deane, *Abstract of British Historical Statistics* (1962), pp. 6–7; *V.C.H. Kent* (1932), Vol. 3, pp. 358f. Eighteenth-century figures of population are based to a considerable extent on Rickman's estimates which have been attacked as inaccurate. For a summary of the present state of the debate on this crucial question of population growth in the 18th century see M. W. Flim, *British Population Growth 1700–1850* (1970).

trade and productivity of labour. This may have been achieved to some degree in the period up to 1801. Certainly more was being spent per head of population on postage though direct comparison is made difficult by complicated rate increases in postages. One point is, however, clear, and that is that despite a rise in postage rates of substantial proportions[70] the amount spent her head of population in Kent fell from 1s. 10.7d. in 1801 to 1s. 8.7d. in 1836. It is unlikely that this was the result of a substantial drop in letter-writing, though the increased rates would most certainly have made people careful not to write unnecessarily. It is much more likely that widespread evasion of these high rates were resorted to.[71]

TABLE XIV

Amount Spent per Head of Population within the County of Kent on Postage

Year	Population	Postal Revenue	Expenditure per head of population
1750	168,679	£3,444	4s. 9d.
1784	247,712	£8,089	7s. 8d.
1800	306,677	£29,671	1s. 10.7d.
1835	506,088	£43,642	1s. 8.7d.

Source: Deane and Cole, *op. cit.*, p. 103; Mitchell and Deane, *op. cit.*, p. 6; P.O.R. Post 3/12; Post 1/12/297; Post 3/18, 3/19, 3/24, 3/25.

Increasing Postal Rates and their Evasion

Palmer's scheme for mail coaches introduced in 1784 was coupled with an increase in postage of a penny on all rates under 150 miles, and 2d. on all rates above this distance. This brought the English rates for a single letter to:

Not exceeding one stage	.. 2d.
Over one but not exceeding two stages	3d.
Up to and including 80 miles	4d.
80 to 150 miles	5d.
Beyond 150 miles in England and Wales	6d.
London to Edinburgh	7d.

Those charges did not last long. As the Napoleonic Wars dragged on, and the need for extra revenue for the Treasury became more urgent, so the postage rates increased. Not only were the existing rates increased, but the rate structure was altered. Increases were made in 1796, 1801, 1805, and again in 1812. The 1812 rates for single letters were:

Not exceeding 15 miles	4d.
15–20 miles	5d.
20–30 miles	6d.
30–50 miles	7d.
50–80 miles	8d.
80–120 miles	9d.
120–170 miles	10d.
170–230 miles	11d.

and so on, the highest rate being 1s. 5d. for above 700 miles.[72] These rates continued unchanged until 1839.

Rising costs during the Napoleonic Wars[73] might have justified increases in postal rates, but those imposed were well in advance of rises for most other commodity prices and wage rates. Table XV lists these increases for postage rates up to 100 miles. In 1812 the price index[74] was 137 points above the base level of 100 set in 1701, but some postage rates had in this period risen by 300 per cent., and all except those for one stage (approximately 10 miles) had risen more than the index of consumer goods. Rates for distances in excess of 100 miles had, if anything risen at an even greater rate. A letter could be carried 300 miles for 3d. in 1700, but in 1812 the same letter would have cost 1s. 0d. Following the cessation of the Napoleonic Wars in 1815 prices began to fall. The overall figure in the Rosseaux price index for 1812 is 196 and this had risen to 203 in 1813. Thereafter it declined, falling by 1833 to 107, though by 1840 it had risen to 128 again. Thus, even if high postage rates were to some degree justified during the War, they were certainly not in the years that followed the cessation of hostilities.[75]

For letters sent from London to destinations in Kent or vice versa, the lowest rate of the 1812 tariff applied only to Footscray and Bromley; Dartford was rated at 5d., Gravesend, Rochester and Sevenoaks at 6d., and Maidstone, Sittingbourne,

TABLE XV

Rise in Postage Rates, 1701–1840

Year	Index of Consumer Goods[1]	Single Letter Rates Exceeding											
		10 miles	%	20 miles	%	40 miles	%	60 miles	%	80 miles	%	100 miles	%
1701[2]	100	2d.	—	2d.	—	2d.	—	2d.	—	2d.	—	3d.	—
1711[3]	135	3d.	50%	3d.	50%	3d.	50%	3d.	50%	3d.	50%	4d.	33.3%
1765[4]	106	1d.	−50%	2d.	—	3d.	50%	3d.	50%	3d.	50%	4d.	33.3%
1784[5]	126	2d.	—	3d.	50%	4d.	100%	4d.	100%	4d.	100%	5d.	66.6%
1796[6]	154	3d.	50%	4d.	100%	4d.	100%	5d.	150%	6d.	200%	6d.	100%
1801[7]	228	3d.	50%	4d.	100%	5d.	150%	6d.	200%	6d.	200%	7d.	133.3%
1805[8]	187	4d.	100%	5d	150%	6d.	200%	7d.	250%	7d.	250%	8d.	166.6%
1812[9]	257	4d.	100%	5d.	150%	7d.	250%	8d.	300%	8d.	300%	9d.	200%

After 1812 postage rates were not revised again until December 1839.

Notes: 1. Mitchell & Deane *op cit* pp. 468-9 (based on Schumpeter-Gilboy price indices). 2. 12 Car. II cap. 35. 3. 9 Anne cap. 10. 4. 5 Geo. III cap. 25. 5. 24 Geo. III Sess. 2 cap. 25. 6. 37 Geo. III cap. 18. 7. 41 Geo. III cap. 8. 45 Geo. III cap. 11. 9. 52 Geo. III cap. 88.

The Isle of Sheppey and Tunbridge Wells paid 7d. Canterbury and other places in the east of Kent were charged 8d., the highest rate being 9d. for Lydd and New Romney. These rates were for single letters, i.e., letters consisting of only one sheet of paper.[76]

The substantial amount of extra revenue expected from the rate increases of 1812 did not materialise. The gross product of the Post Office in the United Kingdom rose from £1,960,510 in 1812 to £2,078,879 in 1813. A peak of £2,418,741 was reached in 1816, but thereafter revenue fell off, and it was not until 1837 that the 1816 figure was again equalled. Evasion was widespread, though those participating quite naturally did not advertise their methods. Much evidence did come to light in 1838, thanks to the investigations of the Select Committee on Postage that was looking into Rowland Hill's scheme for a cheap uniform rate of postage. Rowland Hill himself declared in evidence:

> it is a notorious fact, that all classes of society, from the highest to the lowest, excepting those only who are exempted from postage by Parliamentary or official privilege, frequently send letters by other means than through the Post Office. There is perhaps, scarcely a carriage of any kind, which runs along any of the roads which does not carry a great many: every parcel almost has letters enclosed. Steam boats I know, take enormous numbers of letters, indeed to evade postage, every possible means is resorted to.

Mark Beauchamp Peacock, a Post Office official, when questioned was obliged to admit that

> nothing will prevent the sending illegal letters entirely, and the only means I know of to check the illegal conveyance of letters is by reducing the present rates of postage.[77]

The extent of illegal conveyance in Kent is not easy to estimate, but it was not an unusual occurrence. J. W. Sebright, the Post Office Surveyor, whose area included the county of Kent, when asked about the incidence of illegal conveyance in 1838 stated:

> I am of the opinion that illegal conveyance of letters does prevail in different parts of the country, but I cannot speak positively as to the fact; If I know it to prevail in any particular instance, it would be my duty to bring it forward.

he added later:

> I have no doubt many letters are sent by stage-coaches and carriers
> and by private hands to evade the postage.

Asked if he knew of any illegal conveyance from seaport
towns in his area, he recalled the observations made to him by
the postmaster of Margate:

> that he was surprised that in the season when the population was
> much increased, the postage did not increase in proportion; and he
> seemed to think that it was in consequence of the illegal means of
> conveyance by the steam packets.[78]

When the Margate to Ramsgate twopenny post was set up
in September 1834, one of the reasons for its establishment was
a large-scale loss of letters to carriers and coaches. Before the
reduced rate was introduced, a survey of the number of letters
conveyed in one week was made. Only 33 letters from
Ramsgate to Margate, and 24 from Margate to Ramsgate were
conveyed. The Post Office Surveyor reported:

> It is as you will observe so very trifling that considering the size of
> both Towns and the constant intercourse between them, it is quite
> evident that the bulk of the correspondence goes by other than
> a legal conveyance and I am given to understand it is well known that
> the regular charge for conveying a letter from one town to another
> is 3d.

There were plenty of opportunities for such conveyance,
'Stages passing between the Towns at all hours of the day, the
numerous vans and conveyances of every description by which
letters can be sent'.[79]

Illegal conveyance was notified in East Kent in June 1795
by Mr. Jones, the Surveyor of the Post Horse Duty for Kent,
and in December 1797 it was declared to be considerable
between Sevenoaks and Maidstone, and Ashford and Canterbury.[80]

Where post routes did not exist, no attempt was made to
prevent carriers from conveying letters, but only to or from the
nearest post town. It is probably that this was not strictly
observed, however, and letters were conveyed much further,
for the prevention of conveyance by carriers is often mentioned as one of the advantages to be derived from the setting

up of fifth clause and penny post routes. In December 1816, it was said of the Ashford to Wye penny post that:

> it would prevent the illicit conveyance of letters by means of Carriers & which I fear is now carrying on to a considerable extent notwithstanding our utmost exertions to prevent it.[81]

Free Conveyance of Newspapers and Franks

The profitability of the Post Office was adversely affected by the need to convey free of charge franked newspapers and, after 1836, all newspapers that had paid the obligatory stamp duty. The use of newspapers was one way of evading postage as they could be used to convey messages, but regardless of this, the number of newspapers passing through the post was increasing year by year.

In 1782 there were only 61 newspapers in the British Isles, but this number had increased to 114 in 1790, 216 in 1821, and 369 in 1833. London, by this date, had 13 daily newspapers. The actual number of newspapers dealt with by each post office is known in detail for the period immediately prior to 1840, as the heavy weight of newspapers carried free was one of the points stressed by Rowland Hill and his supporters, and careful surveys were carried out. For earlier periods the evidence is scanty. On 24 June 1801 a count was carried out of all correspondence delivered to outlying villages in the Bromley/Footscray and Sevenoaks areas with a view to providing better deliveries. In the Bromley/Footscray area 148 letters and 51 newspapers were addressed to outlying villages, and in the Sevenoaks area 122 letters and 44 newspapers. This might suggest that about a quarter of the entire mail at this period consisted of newspapers. A virtual monopoly of the distribution of newspapers through the post had been enjoyed by the Clerks of the Roads at the General Post Office before 1764. These were despatched to the provincial postmasters who paid the Clerks 2d. each for them, and were responsible for their local sale.[82] The Clerks of the Roads were still engaged in their distribution in considerable quantity during the first three decades of the 19th century. In a six-month period in the years 1814/5 a total of 98,560 newspapers were despatched by the Clerk of the Kent Road, but by 1829 the total had declined to 132,496 for the whole year. The decline was matched by an

increase in the number of franked newspapers handed to the
Post Office, already addressed by the publishers.

In 1829 the six Clerks of the Roads sent out from London
1,207,794 newspapers, whereas those despatched directly by
the publishers amounted to 10,654,912 in the same year,
nearly nine times as many.[83] Provincial newspapers were also
sent by post in considerable numbers. In the year to 31 October
1837, 1,983 were despatched from Deal, 12,520 from Faversham, and 7,800 from Sevenoaks.[84] More detailed figures exist
for 1838. In the week commencing 15 January 1838, 5,757
newspapers were received by Kentish offices. Of these 924
were accounted for by Canterbury, 316 by Chatham, 814 by
Dover, 481 by Gravesend, and 704 by Maidstone. The total
number of newspapers for the week commencing 29 January
was 5,675. Newspapers appear to have consituted 16.4 per cent.
of all correspondence, but the proportion between letters and
newspapers varied considerably from one post town to another.
It was not the number of the newspapers but their bulk which
gave greatest cause for comparison. On the Hastings Mail
Coach on Tuesday, 3 April 1838 the weight of the letters
was 22lbs. 7ozs., but the newspapers weighed 3qtrs. 25lbs.
Similarly, on the Dover Mail Coah a week later the letters
weighed 1cwt. 1qtr. 7lbs. 3ozs., and the newspapers 2cwts.
6lbs. The greater part of the mail both by weight and bulk was
travelling free.

The Post Office was also saddled with a great volume of
franked letters passing free because of the widespread abuse of
this privilege, especially by Members of Parliament. In the week
commencing 15 January 1838 they represented 9.9 per cent.
of all letters received at Kentish offices. A survey of the mail
carried by the Dover Inland Mail Coach on 10 April 1838
revealed that the coach was carrying 2,291 chargeable letters
on which postage was £77 15s. 0d. The average charge per
letter was 8d., but the cost of conveyance per letter amounted
to 0.7 of a farthing.[85]

Fifth Clause Posts

The majority of new mail routes established in the first 40
years of the 19th century were set up either as local penny

posts or fifth clause posts. Most of the Kentish local posts established in the first decade of the 19th century were under fifth clause regulations. The fifth clause of an Act of 1801 (41 Geo. III, cap. 7) had allowed local posts to be established between outlying villages and the nearest post town at the discretion of the Postmasters-General. The rate to be charged was to be a matter of mutual agreement between the Post Office and the inhabitants of the area to be served. A guarantee of revenue by an important local personage was a great incentive to the setting up of such local posts. In September 1802 Sir William Geary of Oxenheath, near Hadlow, petitioned the Post Office for a direct service from Maidstone to Tonbridge. The post was established under fifth clause regulations, Sir William Geary guaranteeing to the Post Office the sum of £79 2s. 6d. per annum. Rates were fixed at 1d. for a letter and ½d. for a newspaper. It was unusual for fifth clause posts to charge for newspapers, which were not usually subject to general rates of postage, and the charge may subsequently have been dropped. The revenue of the Tunbridge Wells to East Grinstead fifth clause post, which commenced on 23 September 1805, was guaranteed by Lord Whitworth and the Rev. Sackville Beale. In this case the charge for conveyance was much higher. Letters carried the whole 15 miles between the towns were charged at 5d., the usual general post rate. Letters put into the post at either East Grinstead or Tunbridge Wells for one of the intermediate villages were charged at 4d.[86]

No information has come to light to indicate that the guarantors of the fifth clause posts were ever called upon to make up the revenue, though right from the start some of the posts did not cover their costs. On the Dartford to Sevenoaks route for the first six months between 6 August 1804 and 6 February 1805, the revenue for the section as far as Kemsing from fifth clause letters amounted to £29 12s. 6d. To this could be added £1 10s. 7d. in respect of bye letters passing between Dartford and Sevenoaks. Against this total of £31 3s. 1d. were to be set expenses of £32 4s. 0d. (wages of the foot messenger at 19s. per week, and letter receivers at Farningham at £5 5s. 0d. per year; Otford and Kemsing at £3 3s. 0d. per annum each; and Sutton-at-Home £2 2s. 0d. per annum). The Sevenoaks to Kemsing section fared much worse with a revenue from fifth

TABLE XVI

Profitability of Kentish Fifth Clause Posts—Year Commencing 5 July 1835

Office	Routes Operated	Total Revenue			Total Expenses			Profit or Loss		
		£	s.	d.	£	s.	d.	£	s.	d.
Dartford.. : : :	Dartford-Welling	87	18	7	149	6	0	Dr. 61	7	5
	Dartford-Otford									
	Bexley Heath-Welling									
Footscray : : :	Footscray-Chelsfield	24	15	1	55	4	0	Dr. 30	8	11
Lamberhurst : : :	Lamberhurst-Brenchley	96	11	7	55	18	0	40	13	7
Maidstone : : :	Maidstone-Hunton	254	8	2	102	11	0	151	17	2
	Maidstone-Staplehurst									
Tonbridge : : :	Tonbridge-Maidstone	83	11	4	36	8	0	47	3	4
		547	4	9	399	7	0	Cr.147	17	9

Profit on Outlay—27.3 per cent.   Expenses 72.9 per cent. of revenue.

Source: *First Report from the Committee on Postage* (1838) Appendix 25, p. 505ff.

clause letters amounting to only £14 13s. 6d., because some of the inhabitants were still supporting one of the former private messengers. Bye-letters from Sevenoaks to Dartford produced £2 3s. 6d., giving a total revenue of £16 17s. 0d. Expenses, however, were £28 4s. 0d. Despite this loss of £11 7s. 0d., as the revenue was rising the investigating surveyor recommended a continuation for a further 12 months. The losses of the fifth clause posts under Dartford and Footscray were very considerable, though overall for the whole county these posts were reasonably profitable.[87]

Although various sums appear to have been charged for conveyance on fifth clause posts when they were first set up, a standardised charge of a penny appears later to have been accepted. This placed fifth clause posts at a disadvantage when compared with routes operated under penny post regulations. Fifth clause posts were obliged to convey newspapers and franked letters free of charge, whereas the normal penny fee could be charged on penny post routes. It was thus advantageous to the Post Office to convert fifth clause posts into penny posts. This could easily be effected if the number of franked letters handled was small. In July 1839 all existing fifth clause posts were investigated with a view to their conversion to penny posts. Of the three remaining Kentish posts it was found that the Footscray to Orpington and Maidstone to Staplehurst could not be converted because they conveyed 'numerous franks which are at present exempt from charge'. It was feared that 'Great dissatisfaction would be created if now for the first time they were made subject to penny post'.[88]

Penny Posts

A local post system was set up for London in 1680 by William Dockwra as a private commercial undertaking. The fee for carriage was fixed at a penny for each letter or parcel up to a pound in weight. The success of the post speedily led to the prosecution of Dockwra for breaking the Post Office monopoly, and on 19 November 1682 judgement was given against him and the London Penny Post taken under official control. The low postal rate of one penny was not, however,

legalised until the Post Office Act of 1711. The need for such
urban posts outside London was not felt until the middle of
the 18th century. The Post Office Act of 1765[89] made it legal
to organise penny posts 'for any city or town or the suburbs
thereof', and also introduced a General Post rate of a penny
for one stage (usually about 10 or 12 miles). Development of
such posts was slow and even by the end of the century they
existed only in Dublin, Edinburgh, Manchester, Bristol, Birm-
mingham and Glasgow.[90] In the county of Kent, where the
towns were small and the population largely rural, the development of penny posts did not start until 1809, though a number
of postal routes had been opened earlier under the fifth clause
regulations. The slow initial growth can be seen in the following
table:[91]

TABLE XVII

	No. of post towns with penny posts attached	Total number of penny posts routes	Total number of penny posts receiving houses
By 1810	1	1	4
By 1820	7	11	32
By 1830	15	21	65
By 1840	22	39	104

Kentish penny posts connected villages with the nearest post
town, making it unnecessary to go there to collect or post
correspondence. They also established a cheap and efficient
method of local postal communication.[92]
    It would be wrong to assume that, before the penny post
and fifth clause posts, no arrangement existed to supply
outlying villages with letters. A very common method was to
use local carriers. Wye was served by such a carrier prior to
1816 when an official penny post was set up, and the Dover
Road from Canterbury was similarly served. Private foot posts
operated to the villages around Bromley, Chislehurst, Sittingbourne, Wrotham, Walmer, Boughton-under-Blean, Lydd,
Pembury, Westerham, and Whitstable. In some cases the
messenger was employed by the postmaster of the post town

from which he started, who retained any profits that his venture might produce. In other cases the messengers were carrying on the post as an entirely private venture. Some people in the Bromley area had their letters addressed care of local tradesmen, who delivered them free with the orders. The penny post to Brabourne Lees, near Ashford, originated in a military post to the camp set up there during the Napoleonic Wars. Letters to the civilian population along the route were also carried. Thus, even before the establishment of local penny posts, many outlying villages enjoyed a regular postal delivery.[93]

The penny post arrangements in most cases offered a number of advantages over the private methods used before. A regular, and in most cases frequent, service was assured. Penny post routes were operated for six days a week in most cases. Some of the private arrangements provided a less frequent service; e.g., the private letter carrier between Sevenoaks and Wrotham and the surrounding villages only delivered three days a week. As the official penny post messenger was obliged to start at an early hour, and was concerned solely with the delivery of letters, he brought the letters earlier. At Wye, before the penny post from Ashford was set up in 1816, the carrier delivered the letters in the village at 12 noon and was away again an hour later, hardly affording sufficient time for a reply to be sent. The penny post messenger left Ashford at 9 am., arrived at Wye at 10.45 am., and stayed there until 2.45 pm. He arrived back in Ashford in sufficient time for the letters to be stamped, taxed and forwarded by post to Maidstone the same day. Rates of postage at a uniform penny were lower than those charged by most of the private arrangements, some of which required fees as high as 4d. to convey letters from the nearest post town. The most commonly demanded amount was 2d. With many private posts the fee was charged for both letters delivered and those collected for onward transmission by the general post. It was the common practice of the official penny posts to charge only for letters delivered. This enabled posting boxes to be provided. Letters were delivered to any house on the route of the penny post, and in most villages receiving houses were provided at which people who lived away from the direct routes could collect their mail. Being an official arrangement the penny post provided greater security for letters.[94]

In view of the many advantages to be gained by the replacement of the private messenger by penny posts, the conversion was usually welcome. In a few cases, however, the scheme was opposed. In such instances the inhabitants were usually satisfied with their private arrangements. This was the case in March 1839 when the plan for a penny post from Sittingbourne to Milstead was not proceeded with. A similar situation occurred in August 1828 over a proposal to set up a penny post from New Romney to Lydd. In such cases the Post Office did not attempt to impose their scheme. In other cases opposition arose from a concern for the livelihood of the private letter carrier. In the instance of the Deal to Walmer penny post, the only objector was Sir Robert Lee who was anxious to see that the private letter carrier was not left unprovided for and unemployed.[95] Opposition to the setting up of a penny post from Canterbury to Halfway House on the Dover Road in July 1824 came from Sir Henry Oxenden, Mr. W. Foote of Charles Place, and Mr. Hughes Hallet of Higham, who all found the private messenger useful in executing errands. To allay opposition, Arthur Burrows, the private letter carrier, was appointed as the official penny post carrier. As important personages in the area were the largest recipients of letters their views had to receive careful attention when penny post arrangements were being considered. Such people might also be the recipients of numbers of franked letters and newspapers. Such correspondence though free of general postage had to be paid for in the penny post. This was one of the complaints of the people of Broadstairs who, in a memorial sent to the Postmaster-General in March 1830, declared penny postage a 'Tax levied upon them without the authority of Parliament'. In May they went so far as to petition the House of Commons. It is clear that in this case the previous private letter carrier had only charged a penny for which he was willing to deliver letters at either Ramsgate or Margate. The penny post did not proceed beyond Broadstairs, and letters for Margate were routed via Ramsgate and thus paid general postage of 4d. In July 1801 attempts to set up posts from Sevenoaks to Westerham and Wrotham had to

TABLE XVIII

Profitability of the Kentish Penny Posts during their First Year of Operation

Route	Date of Commencement	Surveyor's Estimates			First Year of Operation			References (all Post 42)
		Revenue	Expenses	Profit	Revenue	Expenses	Profit	
		£ s. d.	£ s. d.	£ s. d.	£ s. d.	£ s. d.	£ s. d.	
Sevenoaks–Westerham	1810	156 0 0	49 3 0	106 17 0	124 15 0	56 15 0	68 0 0	101/619 101/132
Maidstone–Sutton Vallance	1816	—	—	—	37 13 0	34 7 0	3 6 0	104/608
Ashford–Brabourne Lees	1816	25 8 0	35 8 0	10 0 0 Dr.	32 2 11	35 8 0	3 5 1 Dr.	104/406 105/180
Ashford–Wye ..	1816	—	33 6 0	Profit expected	33 6 0	33 6 0	—	104/409 105/180
Deal–Walmer ..	1822	—	37 4 0	—	82 10 11	59 17 2	22 13 9	108/50 109/318
Dover–Ewell	1824	54 12 0	38 4 0	16 8 0	47 16 2	36 4 0	11 12 2	110/563 112/455
Faversham–Boughton-under-Blean	1824	44 2 0	38 16 0	5 6 0	39 7 11	36 4 0	3 3 11	110/420 112/455
					397 11 11	292 1 2	105 10 9	

Profit on outlay 36.6%.
Expenses 73.£% of revenue.

TABLE XIX

Profitability of Kentish Penny Posts—Year Commencing 5 July 1835

Office	Routes Operated	Total Revenue £ s. d.			Total Expenses £ s. d.			Profit or Loss £ s. d.		
Ashford	Ashford–Brabourne Lees	84	12	0 ⎫	75	10	0	56	15	7
	Ashford–Wye	47	13	7 ⎭						
Bromley	Bromley–Hayes	36	1	8	37	4	0	1	2	4 Dr.
Canterbury	Canterbury–Halfway House ..	136	17	9 ⎫						
	Canterbury–Whitstable ..	62	10	5 ⎬	207	12	0	156	8	7
	Canterbury–Herne Bay ..	164	12	5 ⎭						
Dartford	Dartford–Swanscombe ..	43	2	3	36	4	0	6	18	3
Deal	Deal–Walmer	44	16	11	35	4	0	9	12	11
Dover	Dover–Ewell	63	13	7	43	8	0	20	5	7
Faversham	Faversham–Boughton ..	46	18	1	36	4	0	10	14	1
Folkestone	Folkestone–Sandgate ..	95	15	7	28	0	0	67	15	7
Gravesend	Gravesend–Northfleet ..	29	12	9	31	0	0	1	7	3 Dr.
Lamberhurst[1]	Hurst Green–Burwash ..	37	14	5 ⎫	86	10	0	45	3	8
	Flimwell–Wadhurst ..	93	19	3 ⎭						

TABLE XIX—*continued*

Office	Routes Operated	Total Revenue £ s. d.	Total Expenses £ s. d.	Profit or Loss £ s. d.
Maidstone	Maidstone–Headcorn	77 2 3		
	Maidstone–Ashford			
	Bearstead	27 17 6		
	Parkgate	44 19 2		
	Harrietsham	19 6 8	286 2 0	41 9 9
	Sandaway	32 4 4		
	Lenham	29 2 6		
	Charing	85 2 8		
	Hoathfield	11 16 8		
Margate	Broadstairs	2 9 0	44 16 0	20 17 4 Dr.
	Ramsgate	21 9 8		
New Romney	New Romney–Brookland	8 16 8	35 6 0	14 19 10
	New Romney–Lydd	41 9 2		
Ramsgate	Broadstairs	3 5 8		
	Margate	19 8 10		
	Broadstairs and Margate	3 9 4	72 0 0	87 5 8
	Broadstairs and Ramsgate	4 15 0		
	St. Peters	128 6 10		
Sevenoaks	Sevenoaks–Wrotham	116 8 0		
	Sevenoaks–Westerham	35 18 0		
	Sundridge			

TABLE XIX—*continued*

		£ s. d.	£ s. d.	£ s. d.
Sevenoaks—*cont.*	Riverhead	43 2 10	150 14 0	240 13 9
	Brasted	43 2 10		
	Westerham	132 18 2		
	Chipstead	23 17 8		
Shooter's Hill[2]	Woolwich	55 11 9	No expense— carried by London District Post on ordinary duties	
	Plumstead			
	New Charlton			
	Eltham			
	Deptford	26 4 11		178 14 1
	New Cross and Peckham	8 15 8		
	Blackheath			
	Lewisham			
	Lee	88 2 1		
	Greenwich			
	Old Charlton			
Sittingbourne	Sittingbourne-Rainham	73 16 9	102 13 0	66 16 11
	Sittingbourne-Doddington	95 13 2		
Tonbridge	Tonbridge-Pembury	52 4 0	47 3 0	42 1 7
	Tonbridge-Penshurst	37 0 7		
		2,377 8 11	1,355 10 0	1,022 8 11

Profit on outlay 75.4%.   Expenses 57% of revenue.   Source: *First Report from the Select Committee on Postage* (1838), Appendix 24, p. 474.

Notes.—1. Largely serving places in Sussex. 2. Mail from Dover Road for N.W. Kent (now S.E. London) unloaded at Shooter's Hill to save the need to take it to Central London before entering London District Post.

be abandoned because of opposition from the private letter carriers themselves, who threatened to compete with any official post set up, and cut their rates to a half penny if necessary.[96]

The Post Office saw in the penny posts a valuable additional source of revenue. Not only did the pence collected in virtually every case exceed the cost of running the post but they also made it more convenient for people who did not live in post towns to receive and send letters through the general post. By transferring the carriage of letters from private to official hands it helped to discourage illegal conveyance of letters.

Penny posts were usually set up on the advice of the resident Post Office Surveyor for the area, and normally were only established if the route would be of benefit to the postal revenue. The profitability of the proposed route was not hard to assess. A check at the post town from which the delivery was to originate of the number of letters and newspapers for addresses on the proposed route would give an accurate idea of the revenue. The main expense of a penny post was the messenger, whose weekly pay would depend on the length of the route and the hours of duty. Apart from this there would be the need to employ a receiver at most villages to take in letters at his cottage from inhabitants off the route of the letter carrier. Petitions were also forwarded to the Post Office by the inhabitants of villages who wished for penny post delivery. These were usually granted only if the number of letters suggested that the post would be profitable. Some suggested routes like those from Faversham to Boughton-under-Blean, and Tonbridge to Pembury were refused when initially suggested, but later were opened; an indication of the increasing volume of correspondence.[97]

A comparison of the profitability of the penny posts in the year in which they were established with the year ending 5 July 1836, by which time several of them had been functioning for 20 years or more, is revealing. Not only were these posts by 1836 performing a useful service at a low cost to the community they served, but they were also providing a valuable and increasing source of revenue to the Post Office. Their superiority in profitability over the fifth clause posts, where newspapers and franks were allowed to pass free, was marked.

TABLE   XX

	Year Ending 5 July 1836	
	Profit on outlay	% of expenses to revenue
Kentish Penny Posts	75.4%	57%
Kentish Fifth Clause Posts	37.3%	72.9%[98]

In the year ending 5 July 1836 only two penny posts were making a loss. In both cases these had been recently established and the loss was insignificant. They could be expected to make a profit in the years to come. Fifth clause posts attached to both Dartford and Footscray were in the same year making very considerable losses.[99] Although the profitability of the penny posts appear substantial, it did not compare favourably with that of the postal services as a whole, for in the year ending 5 January 1836, a nett profit of £1,564,458 was made, the expenses being a mere £678,836.

Post Office profits were from the end of the Napoleonic Wars virtually static. In the year ending 5 January 1814 the profit of £1,506,064 was much the same as that for the year ending 5 January 1836.[100]   The penny posts were however increasing their profitability.

TABLE XXI

Penny Post route	First year of operation			Year ending 5 July 1836		
	£	s.	d.	£	s.	d.
Sevenoaks–Westerham	68	0	0	240	13	9
Ashford–Brabourne Lees	3	5	1 Dr.	56	15	7
Ashford–Wye	not known					
Deal–Walmer	22	13	9	9	12	11
Dover–Ewell	11	12	2	20	5	7
Faversham–Boughton	3	3	11	10	14	1
	£102	4	9[101]	£338	1	11

Although the sample taken is small, as other comparable figures are not available, the rise in profitability is sharp. It might be argued that the figure for the first year of operation were not a fair comparison, but it must be remembered that in all the examples used a local postal system did exist prior to the setting up of the official penny post. In the case of Ashford to Brabourne Lees it was an official arrangement, in the other cases private but regular delivery, which in the case of the Sevenoaks to Westerham route was controlled by the Sevenoaks postmaster.[102]

Commenting upon the penny posts, Dr. Howard Robinson states:

> The grasping Post Office had thought, for a time that it had the power to make these penny posts into twopenny posts, and some few were established on this basis.

This statement would seem to imply an attempt to increase the rates on existing penny posts purely to bring in increased revenue. These twopenny posts appear to have been entirely new establishments set up between post towns near to one another, on letters between which general rates of postage had been previously charged. After 1812 the lowest general rate was 4d. The only example of a twopenny post in Kent was that set up between Ramsgate and Margate in September 1834. Prior to this, similar posts had been set up between Plymouth and Devonport, Portsmouth and Gosport, and in several places in Scotland, the earliest dating from 1831. The Ramsgate to Margate twopenny post was set up because the 4d. postage rate was too high to attract the bulk of the letters, which were being conveyed illegally by a variety of methods. At the reduced rate of 2d., and by the introduction of three posts a day, the Post Office hoped not only to stop the illegal conveyance, but to increase profitability. In March 1837 the twopenny charge was discontinued outside London as there was no legal sanction for it.[103]

Parts of North-west Kent enjoyed cheaper postage, as they were included within the boundaries of the London District Post. From its foundation in 1680 up to 1794 the charge had been 1d. for letters in Central London and 2d. for outlying areas. A penny extra was added to both rates in 1794. Contained in the outer 3d. area in Kent were the settlements and suburbs of Beckenham, Blackheath, Charlton, Eltham

Greenwich, Lee, New Cross, Plumstead, Shooter's Hill, Syden-
ham, and Woolwich. The inhabitants of Bromley were anxious
to be included, but applications were rejected in both 1810
and 1817 on the grounds that revenue would be lost, and the
villages between Bromley and Sevenoaks left without a postal
service. From 1806 the lowest general post rate was 4d.

In 1833 it was decided to alter the boundary of the London
District Post. Previously it had been irregular in shape, now it
was to be a circle with a radius 12½ miles from the G.P.O.
at St. Martin's-le-Grand. This considerably increased the area
served, and from 9 November 1833 Bromley, Bexley, Chislehurst, Crayford, Erith, Footscray, Hayes, The Crays, Sidcup,
Welling, and East and West Wickham were included within the
new boundary. This brought the boundary to within three miles
of Dartford, whose inhabitants petitioned to be included in
the extended London District Post, but in February 1834 their
request was refused. The general post offices at Bromley and
Footscray continued to operate for the reception of general
post letters, those for the London District Post being handled
separately. As letters for London addresses were now sent by
the cheaper London District Post, the new arrangement led to
a decline in the amount of general post revenue derived from
these two offices.[104]

Theft and Security of the Mails

One of the reasons for the introduction of the mail coaches
was the added security that they gave the mails. Palmer's
original plan was that the coaches should be guarded by a
soldier. This was found to be impracticable, but the mail
coach guard, who was a Post Office employee, was provided
with a cutlass, a brace of pistols, and a blunderbuss, which
were inspected by the Post Office armourer before each
journey. These measures effectively put an end to the holding
up of mail on those roads served by mail coaches.[105] The
mail carts and riders, however, were still vulnerable. Francis
Freeling advocating the guarding of such mails wrote in
March 1796:

> It seems to be the unanimous opinion that the person who conveys
> the Mail should be equal to the protection of it. That it would be

improper and dangerous to entrust the use of Fire Arms to the present description of Riders, many of whom are barely 14 years of age. That none but persons of good character, above 18 and not exceeding 45 years of age should be employed, and that with persons of this description properly armed the defence of the Mails would in all probability be compleat.

It was suggested that all riders 'should be furnished with cutlass, brace of pistols' and a 'strong cap for the defence of his head'. Treasury consent was given in December 1801 for all horse posts and mail carts to be provided with armed protection, the amount allocated for this purpose being £1,500 per annum. One of the first Kentish posts to be protected was that from Rochester to Maidstone in September 1802. Where mail carts were in use guards were appointed. The guard of the Rochester to Maidstone mail cart in June 1806 was paid 10s. 6d. a week. Foot posts were also armed. In 1811 when the Hawkhurst to Tenterden horse post was replaced by two foot posts they were provided with arms. Francis Freeling commented that 'an able armed foot messenger will better protect the Bags than a Boy on a Pony'. In 1813 all Kentish riders were armed, with the exception of those between Tonbridge and Tunbridge Wells, Maidstone and Ashford, and Maidstone and Tonbridge. The situation was the same in January 1824, except that Tonbridge to Tunbridge Wells was now a foot post, and the new foot post between Margate and Ramsgate was also not armed. The protection of the posts in this manner was a deterrent to robbers along the highway.[106]

When giving evidence upon the feasibility of Palmer's plan to set up mail coaches, Mr. Draper, one of the Post Office Surveyors, declared that 'experience has shown that no invention can prevent desperate fellows'. He further declared that when such persons had decided to rob the mails the only consequence of arming those responsible for its conveyance 'would be murder in case of resistance'.[107] In practice few attempts were made to stop mail coaches and those made were unsuccessful. In Kent no such attempts were made at all. Two cases are known of theft of mails from mail coaches, but both occurred because the guard left the mails unattended. The first of these happened on the night of Tuesday, 6 June 1826 between Chatham and Rainham when several bags were taken.

The guard instead of travelling at the back where the mail bags were kept in a locked box, went to the front of the coach close to the coachman.[108] A few months later, on the night of 29 January 1827, the Naples bag was stolen while the mail coach was left unattended at Canterbury during a change of horses.[109]

Highway robbery of mails conveyed by riders and mail carts continued at a level that caused alarm to the Post Office until armed protection was provided. In August 1786 the post boy conveying the foreign mails from Dover was attacked near Canterbury and two of the bags broken open.[110] The Rye and Hastings mail was attacked several times in the Farnborough area between July 1798 and March 1801, while the Maidstone to Ashford rider was stopped and threatened by a footpad on the morning of 16 September 1798 near Charing. It is significant that all these robberies took place before armed protection was provided for the mails. In the period from 1802 onwards, no mails appear to have been held up on the roads in Kent with intention to steal the mail, with one possible exception. Baines in his book *On the Track of the Mail Coach* records that a post boy with the foreign mails from Dover was held up and robbed near Canterbury in August 1814. The mails were not touched, and there is no indication that the boy was armed. A theft of mail bags from the mail cart between Rye and Northiam occurred on 20 January 1824, but there is no indication that the cart was held up.[111]

The attraction of the mail to the thief was the letters containing coin or notes. These also could be a temptation to the staff engaged in their transit. Loss of letters and the fraud and neglect found upon investigation led to the dismissal of the postmasters of Chatham (March 1794), Rochester (February 1796), Gravesend (July 1800), Wingham (September 1815), and New Romney (December 1835), and also the receiver at Goudhurst (December 1811).[112] Letter carriers were tempted to steal letters which they knew contained coins or notes. The letter carrier employed between Tonbridge and Southborough was arrested in December 1824 for embezzling a letter containing a guinea. In March 1830 the penny post messenger from Ashford to Brabourne Lees absconded with a letter containing five sovereigns, the postage money collected by him, and the salaries of the Brabourne and Mersham receivers that had been entrusted to him for delivery. Other cases in contemporary documents are mainly concerned with the theft of individual letters in transit or from post offices. Usually such letters contained money or banknotes. Where the negligence could be attributed to an individual postmaster he might be expected to pay compensation for the loss. For the period 1774 to 1836, 387 prosecution briefs exist in the Post Office Records Office concerned with offences against the mails. Of these 12 refer to the county of Kent. Eight of the persons prosecuted were employed in the despatch and delivery of the mails in one capacity or another.[113]

At times mail bags were lost by accident, having fallen from the coach, cart of post boy's horse. Rewards were offered for their recovery. When in October 1838 the Bromley, Tonbridge and Sevenoaks bags were lost by the guard of the Hastings and St. Leonards Mail Coach a reward of £5 was offered. Such rewards were only paid if the bags were taken to the nearest post office immediately they were found. In two cases where mail bags were lost in Kent, the finders were country labourers who failed to realise the significance or what they had found or the correct line of action to be taken. On 9 May 1825 the London to Deal bag was lost near Canterbury and a reward of £20 offered for its return 'contents safe'. The bag was found on the night of the 9th by a waggoner who failed to take it to the Canterbury post office until the morning of the 12th. In another instance when a bag was lost near Chalk, Edward Bowen, the finder, not only detained the bag, but opened it before handing it in at Gravesend post office. On examination before a magistrate it was discovered that he was not aware of what he had found as he could not read. Post Office employees, contractors or their servants who lost letter bags were usually made to pay the cost incurred in their recovery.[114]

Delay could be caused in the winter by snow and severe weather. Communication between the Isle of Sheppey and the mainland was cut in January 1795. On the 16th the postmaster at Queenborough reported that:

> The greatest exertion has been made to the great Hazard of Lives to get the Mail forward, but the very great fall of Snow today and still continuing renders every effort vain at present.

Six days later the Sittingbourne postmaster indicated that the ferry had stopped and the mails could not be forwarded. On the 26th mail was conveyed over the ice. Almost immediately after the thaw set in. It was particularly frustrating in time of war to have military installations cut off in this manner. Coaches were particularly badly affected by heavy snow falls. On 7 December 1816 Francis Freeling requested Lord Sidmouth, the Home Secretary, to instruct parish authorities, through the Lords Lieutenant of the counties and the magistrates 'to use every means of clearing the Roads in the event of a fall of Snow and thereby prevent any Impediment to the regular Conveyance of the Mails'. It was thought that requests solely by local postmasters would not carry much weight. East Kent was particularly affected by heavy winter snowfalls. Coaches on the Dover Road were suspended from 25 to 31 December 1836 and during the particularly severe winter of 1836/7 an additional payment of £5 5s. 0d. each was made to the contractors for the Canterbury to Margate and Canterbury to Ramsgate riders for their exertions in conveying the mails.[115]

Accidents also delayed postal traffic. These were caused either by defects in the carts or carriages or the state of the road in most cases, but more bizarre examples were also to be found. In August 1798 one of the horses pulling the Dover Mail Coach over Rochester bridge was struck by lightning, while on 22 September 1824 the Hastings Mail coach was overturned in Tonbridge High Street after striking a heap of manure that had been left in the roadway.[116]

In the case of accidents the drivers of mail carts, riders and foot posts had no right to any assistance from the Post Office if injured. They conveyed the mails, but were employed not by the Post Office but by the contractor or postmaster. In cases when Post Offices employees such as mail coach guards sustained accidents in the course of duty, they were entitled to five guineas as a surgeon's fee and 10s. 6d. a week until fit for duty. This was at times allowed to the servants of contractors, but never as a right. In September 1820 Thomas Parks, the driver of the Maidstone to Tonbridge Mail Cart, was thrown from it in the course of his duties, and broke his leg. He was allowed 10s. 6d. a week, but this ceased in

January 1821 when the leg failed to heal and the Post Office refused to settle the surgeon's account as he was not a Post Office employee. Stephen Firth, contractor for the Maidstone to Tonbridge ride, was also paid 10s. 6d. a week when his wrist was dislocated in October 1825 in a similar accident. A claim made in June 1839 by the Maidstone to Sutton Valence letter carrier that his illness was aggravated 'by the exercise of walking' was rejected and it was stated that relief could only be given 'in cases of positive injury arising from sudden cause or accident while in the discharge of duty'.[117]

Reports of negligence by postal employees seem less in evidence than at earlier periods. Apart from the postmasters dismissed for negligence or fraud, and some cases of theft mentioned previously,[118] other references are few. Some drunkenness existed, but this was not to be wondered at in mail guards whose stopping places were usually inns. The only example noted for Kent is that of John Carter, the guard on Palmer's first coach to Bath, but later because of drink transferred to the least lucrative of the mail coach routes, the Dover Foreign Mail, where in the period following the outbreak of the war with Revolutionary France, passengers and tips were few. When this coach was withdrawn in 1795, he was used as an extra guard when required. The severe weather of January 1795, and the resulting illness, led to his being used on the Dover Inland Mail, where he disgraced himself by reverting to his old ways and losing the Gravesend bag.

A further case of drunkenness on duty occurred in August 1795. After the mail from Hastings had become overdue three or four hours, the Postmaster of Bromley set off down the road to find out what had happened to it. He discovered that the rider had stopped at a public house to drink with some friends. The Post Office ordered that the rider be prosecuted, and if convicted, the case publicised in the newspapers as a warning to others. In August 1827 the repeated lateness of the Maidstone to Yalding fifth clause post letter carrier led to his dismissal, though he was reinstated for a trial period as he had a family and a blind wife to support.

On the other hand there were employees who had given many years of faithful service, like Edmund Blake of Tunbridge Wells, who had been employed by the postmaster in the town for 20 years and was still in employment in April 1834. No form of pension could be expected by such persons, who were deemed to be employed by the postmaster and not the Post Office. When in June 1834 a memorial from the leading citizens of Margate was sent to the Postmaster-General in support of 'a small Allowance by way of Annuity or Superannuation' for James Taylor, many years letter carrier at Margate, the Post Office refused to help, merely hoping that those who had signed the memorial would be able to provide assistance.[119]

Chapter 5

KENTISH POSTMASTERS, 1784-1840

IN CHARGE of postal affairs in each post town was the 'deputy postmaster' who usually owed his appointment to influence. When a vacancy occurred in a post town, it was the nominee of the local members of parliament who was usually appointed. At Hythe in February 1800 it was the nominee of the two M.P.s for the borough who was made postmaster, while in January 1796 the vacancy at Rochester was filled on the recommendation of Sir E. Knatchbull, one of the county M.P.s, and Mr. Best, one of the borough M.P.s. The Duchess of Dorset was concerned with the appointments at Sevenoaks in December 1797 and at Tonbridge in March 1810. Less influential persons might also express their views. When the nominee of the Duchess of Dorset refused the Tonbridge appointment, the nominee of Mr. Children, a Tonbridge banker, was given the position. With the smaller offices where the salary was less, the status of those recommending appointments appears to have been less exalted. At Wingham in January 1802, the maiden sister of the previous postmistress was appointed on the recommendation of the Post Office surveyor. The salary of this post office was however only £10 per annum.[1]

The qualifications necessary to obtain such a post were never formally laid down. In the larger post towns it was a position of considerable responsibility and required a good education and a degree of organising ability. When Sir William Curtis wrote to Francis Freeling on 24 November 1816 with a view to obtaining employment for a protégé as postmaster of Ramsgate, he declared:

> I have a nice fellow, native of this place, a son of a Lieutenant of the Navy and of examplary character, and one above all other men I wish to provide for, he has had a good education at Christ's Hospital.

The appointment of incompetent and near illiterate persons as deputies could cause considerable confusion and difficulty. In May 1810 complaints were made against the postmistress of Wingham, who was declared by the Accountant of the Bye Letter Office to be either totally inattentive or incompetent. She was dismissed as her inaccuracy in accounts was destroying their value as a check on other offices.[2]

During the 17th and most of the 18th centuries postmasters had also been innkeepers and responsible for finding post boys and horses. With the coming of the mail coaches and the widespread use of mail carts, riding contracts were put out to tender, and no longer was it necessary for a postmaster to be an innkeeper. In October 1792 the Post Office in fact declared itself against the appointment of innkeepers as this resulted in a lack of security for the mails. Separate rooms for postal business were seldom provided by such persons, and it might well be conducted at the bar. By March 1836 only one post town in the whole county had an innkeeper as a postmaster, though one other was declared to be a licensed victualler, another a wine merchant, and two others brewers. Other trades represented were broker, newspaper agent, druggist, ironmonger, watchmaker, hatter, purser R.N., plumber, stationer and bookseller, and grocer. The largest group appears to have been newsagents, stationers and booksellers, the post-masters of Canterbury, Sheerness, Tonbridge, Tunbridge Wells, Sittingbourne, and Tenterden all being of these trades. In 10 cases the postmasters were declared to have no other trade. Some of these offices, such as Dover and Ramsgate, were important with large salaries, where clearly the post office provided full-time employment. Others were quite small places, such as Wingham and New Romney where the salaries and perquisites were much lower. In a town like Tunbridge Wells the possession of the post office was considered of very great value. In May 1822 the District Surveyor, Mr. Scott, found that the postmaster, Jasper Sprange, did not visit the post office more than once or twice a week. The office was not at his house, but situated in a library run by John Elliott. Sprange drew the salary while Elliott was content to do the work for nothing. Mr. Scott commented:

the emoluments it should seem are a secondary consideration to him, his first object in possessing the office being the inducement it holds out to visitors and others to become subscribers to his library.

On Sprange's death in 1823 there was a tussle between John Elliott and John Nash, another library proprietor, for the appointment.[3]

Women were appointed postmistresses or allowed to take over on the death of a husband. Of the 29 Kentish post towns in March 1836, four had postmistresses. One of these was the important Ramsgate office, the salary and emoluments of which were £178 16s. 0d. per annum. When a postmistress married it was the ruling of the Post Office that she must give up the appointment, but it could be transferred to the husband. At Faversham, the widow of Mr. Plowman, the late postmaster, took over on his death, but in 1800 she married Andrew Hill who became postmaster in her place. His period of office was short, for he died in July of the same year and Sarah Hill was reappointed. In June 1801 she announced her intended marriage to Mr. Lamprey and asked once more for the office to be transferred.[4]

The hours of work demanded from the postmasters were long and in most offices the duties were heavy. Attention was needed constantly and they were expected to live under the same roof as their office. Postmasters were expected to supervise the work and were not permitted to appoint a deputy to do it for them. This ruling was pointed out to Stephen Kemsley, the postmaster of Ashford, in April 1793. At this date he appears to have been permanently living at Maidstone. Duties at the Maidstone office were not untypical of those undertaken by postmasters in the larger towns. These commenced at 3.30 am. with the arrival of the London letters from Rochester. An hour later the letters arrived from Tonbridge. These had to be sorted for the town deliveries and for West Malling, Yalding, Staplehurst, Ashford, and Sutton Valence routes. The post office itself opened at 7 am. in the summer and 8 am. in the winter. Duties did not end until 10 pm., and in May 1830 were sufficient to provide employment for three members of the postmaster's family. Of the Sittingbourne postmaster it was stated in June 1836 that he had not throughout the night a clear interval of two hours to devote to rest. To assist the postmasters, allowances had been made by 1836 for a clerk at Canterbury, Chatham, Dover (part-time), Gravesend, Lamberhurst, Margate, Ramsgate, and Sevenoaks. Clerks paid by the postmasters were additionally employed at Bromley, Chatham, Deal, Dover, Gravesend (two part-time), Hythe, Rochester, Tonbridge, and Tunbridge Wells. Allowances for salaries for the clerks varied from £60 per annum for Deal to £6 per annum for Tonbridge.[5]

Letter boxes appear to have been provided at most offices for the receipt of unpaid letters. Certainly these were provided at Folkestone, Hythe, New Romney, Margate, Lamberhurst, and Tunbridge Wells. Even at places that were not post towns such as Strood, Sandgate, and Whitstable, the receiving office had a post box. Boxes were only provided at the offices, and these were closed at a convenient time before the departure of the mails. In December 1839 the Tunbridge Wells box was normally closed at 9 pm. This office appears to have been provided with a box as early as 1786 for London letters, but at this date foreign and cross-post letters had to be handed to the postmaster or a member of his staff.[6]

The postmasters were responsible for dispatching the money taken in postage to the General Post Office in London. A notice instructed all persons sending remittances by post to divide notes payable to bearer into two, and advised their despatch by two separate posts. This routine was followed on 11 December 1825 by the Gravesend postmaster who sent half notes to the value of £80 of Messrs. Becket & Co., bankers of Gravesend to the Post Office as settlement. The other halves were sent on 13 December, the day that payment on the notes was stopped. Only 12s. 0d. in the pound was able to be paid from the assets of the bank, but the Post Office credited the balance of £32 to the postmaster's account as it was their instructions regarding the forwarding of remittances that had caused the loss.[7]

Postmasters were the eyes and ears of the government and were instructed to send 'an immediate Account of all remarkable occurrances within their districts, that the same may be communicated to His Majesty's Principal Secretary of State'.

They shared this responsibility with other government employees, and during the Napoleonic Wars, when the Post Office no longer had a packet establishment or agent at Dover, the customs service played an active part in detecting illegal conveyance of mail, and especially attempts to bring letters in from overseas. In January 1794 a number of letters 'addressed to sundry French Persons now in London' were seized from passengers on the Dover Coach by customs officials and forwarded to the Secretary of State. The postmasters of Gravesend, Deal, Dartford, and Canterbury were directed in June 1797, during the trial of Richard Parker and other delegates after the mutiny at The Nore, to send all letters passing between ships lying at Greenhithe and Sheerness and those at The Downs to the Post Office in London in case they were 'of signficance'. A warrant was issued on 16 August 1798 to detain the letters of Mr. F. Andrews of Folkestone, Mr. J. Burt of Packington and Mr. Tharkey of Lydd. How many similar warrants were issued for Kent or how many letters opened without warrant is not known, but in 1844 it was stated that only 372 such warrants naming 724 persons had been issued for the United Kingdom from 1799 to 1844, and only 101 from 1712 to 1798. The highest number issued for a single year was 28 in 1812.[8]

The reports of local occurrences sent in by Kentish post-masters often appear trivial compared with those of other towns especially in the Midlands and the North, who reported regularly on local acts of violence and on groups of workmen who were trying to organise for political or economic ends. The Chatham postmaster in January 1821 commented upon a handbill announcing opposition to the divorce proceedings against the Queen, which was being distributed locally, and also a letter of denunciation sent to the Archdeacon of Rochester on the same theme. During the disturbances at the time of the passing of the First Reform Bill in 1832, the postmaster of Sheerness was on 12 April concerned to report a fire that had broken out in a cabinet maker's house in the night, while the Chatham postmaster on 28 May mentioned indiscipline amongst the soldiers of the garrison. Both Canterbury and Faversham postmasters in May 1838 reported a riot that had broken out at Boughton.[9]

Not all postmasters performed their duties to the satis-
faction of the Post Office authorities and a number were
dismissed. The most common causes of dismissal were
neglect of duties, peculation, falsification of accounts and
debt. Often elements of all these were present in the situation
that led to the dismissal. Debt and peculation often went
hand in hand. As early as 1793 the Chatham postmaster,
Mr. Maclean, was seriously in arrears. In February 1794
investigation revealed attempts to overcharge letters and
retain the extra collected for his own use. His successor,
William Allen, was £600 in debt to the Post Office by April
1797, and in May was committed to Maidstone gaol. A further
attempt at fraud in May 1813 led to the dismissal of yet
another Chatham postmaster. The Sittingbourne postmaster
in March 1799 did not wait to be dismissed after investigations into the opening of a letter containing money. He fled
and the Post Office subsequently printed 2,000 bills offering
a reward for his apprehension. A thorough investigation
revealed 'one continued system of Fraud in the office at
Sittingbourne', and the postmaster was apprehended and
put on trial.[10]

The salaries paid to postmasters often appear low, but
could be augmented by various perquisites and emoluments,
which for some offices amounted to more than the salary
itself. These included local delivery fees, late posting fees,
gratuities in respect of private box facilities, and profits on
money orders. The number and extent of these private and
semi-private ventures tended to decrease, especially in the
field of local delivery, forcing the Post Office to pay more
adequate salaries. Between 1791 and 1838 the salaries of
Kentish postmasters rose on an average 385 per cent., ranging
from a mere 117 per cent. for Queensborough to 767 per
cent. for Rochester.[11] Salaries were examined with a view
to their increase as a result of a recommendation by the Post
Office Surveyor for the district. The investigation may have
originated in a petition for an increase forwarded from the
postmaster himself. On 15 August 1832 Mr. Scott, the Surveyor, reported that the duties of the Sevenoaks office included
much night work, and made the employment of assistance
essential for the proper performance of duties.

TABLE XXII

Increase in Postmasters' Salaries, 1791–1838

Office	1791			1838			Increase			Percentage Increase
	£	s.	d.	£	s.	d.	£	s.	d.	%
Ashford	6	0	0	50	0	0	44	0	0	733
Bromley	20	0	0	58	10	0	38	10	0	193
Canterbury ..	40	0	0	140	0	0	100	0	0	250
Cranbrook ..	6	0	0	35	0	0	29	0	0	483
Dartford.. ..	12	0	0	90	0	0	78	0	0	650
Deal	30	0	0	152	0	0	122	0	0	470
Dover	30	0	0	90	0	0	60	0	0	200
Faversham ..	8	0	0	52	0	0	44	0	0	550
Footscray ..	6	0	0	34	0	0	28	0	0	467
Gravesend ..	20	0	0	70	0	0	50	0	0	250
Hythe	8	0	0	54	0	0	46	0	0	575
Lamberhurst ..	12	0	0	78	0	0	66	0	0	550
Maidstone ..	12	0	0	80	0	0	68	0	0	567
Margate	18	0	0	70	0	0	52	0	0	289
New Romney ..	8	0	0	36	0	0	28	0	0	350
Queenborough..	12	0	0	26	0	0	14	0	0	117
Rochester ..	12	0	0	104	0	0	92	0	0	767
Sandwich ..	6	0	0	40	0	0	34	0	0	567
Sevenoaks ..	16	0	0	66	10	0	50	10	0	291
Sittingbourne ..	12	0	0	50	0	0	38	0	0	317
Tenterden ..	6	0	0	30	0	0	24	0	0	400
Tonbridge .. ⎱ Tunbridge Wells ⎰	16	0	0	⎰80 ⎱56	0 0	0 0	120	0	0	750
	316	0	0	1,542	0	0	1,226	0	0	385

Sources: P.O.R. Post 9/131, 9/132.

The salary of the postmaster was only £50, and from this had to be deducted office expenses of £10. On £40 a year he could not afford an assistant. The revenue of the office was stated to be £1,900 per annum. an increase of £30 in salary was allowed commencing from 5 July to be paid on indents until Treasury approval was received.[12]

The courts had in 1772 ruled that it was illegal to levy charges for delivery within a post town, but where the population did not complain these local delivery charges continued.

TABLE XXIII

Salaries and Emoluments of the Kentish Postmasters for the Year Ending 1 March 1836 and their Relationship to the Revenue of the Office

Office	Salary	Total Emoluments and Perquisites			Total Income			Revenue[1] of the Office			Remarks
	£	£	s.	d.	£	s.	d.	£	s.	d.	
Ashford	44	7	0	0	51	0	0	1,047	5	0	
Bromley (General Post only)	58	5	10	0	63	10	0	390	4	4	Plus £20 salary from the London District Post
Canterbury	140	120	13	9	260	13	9	4,383	14	10	
Chatham	58	46	0	0	104	0	0	2,887	3	1	Compensation of £60 also paid
Cranbrook	35	1	5	0	36	5	0	621	11	3	
Dartford..	66	10	0	0	76	0	0	1,349	19	2	
Deal	140	16	0	0	156	0	0	716	12	4	
Dover	90	79	18	6	169	18	6	3,607	5	9	
Faversham	52	30	0	0	82	0	0	1,001	14	4	
Folkestone	46	5	0	0	51	0	0	798	9	3	
Footscray (General Post only)	34	8	2	0	42	2	0	173	18	4	Plus £5 salary from the London District Post
Gravesend	50	27	5	3	77	5	3	1,848	4	8	
Hythe	54	5	0	0	59	0	0	582	15	9	

TABLE XXIII.—*continued.*

Office	Salary	Total Emoluments and Perquisites			Total Income			Revenue[1] of the Office			Remarks
	£	£	s.	d.	£	s.	d.	£	s.	d.	
Lamberhurst .. ::	78	3	8	0	81	8	0	1,972	17	2	
Maidstone ::	80	95	12	6	175	12	6	5,016	1	8	
Margate .. ::	70	100	19	4½	170	19	4½d.	2,170	6	3	
New Romney .. ::	36	3	18	0	39	18	0	360	4	8	
Queenborough.. ::	26	0	10	0	26	10	0	211	6	8	
Ramsgate ::	120	56	16	0	178	16	0	3,430	17	5	Plus £50 compensation
Rochester ::	104	166	10	0	270	10	0	1,837	1	6	
Sandwich ::	40	1	13	6	41	13	6	560	12	10	
Sevenoaks ::	50	8	0	0	58	0	0	1,867	6	1	
Shooters Hill .. ::	40	—			40	0	0				
Sittingbourne ::	86	10	0	0	96	0	0	1,179	8	8	
Tenterden ::	30	0	14	0	30	14	0	421	0	9	
Tonbridge ::	80	5	0	0	85	0	0	1,854	17	3	
Tunbridge Wells ::	56	71	9	0	127	19	0	2,408	8	1	
Wingham ::	30	6	0	0	36	0	0	459	2	3	

Note.—1. Year ending 5 January 1836.

Sources: P.O.R. Post 3/24, 3/25; *H.C. Sessional Papers 1836* (111.) LV. 373.

TABLE XXIV

Emoluments and Perquisites—Kentish Postmasters—Year Ending 5 January 1837

Office	Compensation for Loss of Perquisites			Private Delivery Letter Boxes			Fees on Late Letters			Profits from the Delivery of Letters			Gratuities			Profits on Money Orders		
	£	s.	d.	£	s.	d.	£	s.	d.	£	s.	d.	£	s.	d.	£	s.	d.
Ashford ..	—			—			3	0	0	1	0	0	3	0	0	1	0	0
Bromley ..	15	0	0	6	6	0	0	5	0	4	3	0	—			1	5	0
Canterbury	60	0	0	—			31	1	5	64	7	7	13	0	0	10	0	0
Chatham	—			8	0	0	9	2	0	15	12	0	—			24	8	4
Cranbrook	—			—			1	10	0	0	5	0	—			—		
Dartford..	—			—			4	0	0	4	0	0	2	2	0	1	0	0
Deal	60	0	0	—			11	0	0	1	10	0	—			4	10	0
Dover ..	4	0	0	—			7	0	0	106	5	0	4	4	0	7	3	4
Faversham	—			—			9	2	6	12	12	0	5	0	0	2	12	0
Folkestone	—			—			2	0	0	0	5	0	2	2	0	2	4	0
Footscray	—			—			0	6	0	—			—			—		
Gravesend	—			—			4	0	0	87	10	0	0	10	0	5	5	0
Hythe ..	—			—			3	0	0	1	10	0	2	0	0	1	14	0
Lamberhurst ..	—			—			2	2	0	0	13	0	2	12	0	—		

TABLE XXIV.—*continued.*

Office	Compensation for Loss of Perquisites £ s. d.	Private Delivery Letter Boxes £ s. d.	Fees on Late Letters £ s. d.	Profits from the Delivery of Letters £ s. d.	Gratuities £ s. d.	Profits on Money Orders £ s. d.
Maidstone	—	—	25 0 0	46 8 6	16 16 0	2 0 0
Margate	—	—	12 3 0	2 12 0	6 2 0	—
New Romney	—	—	0 8 0	0 2 3	—	1 14 9
Queenborough.. ..	30 0 0	—	0 10 0	0 3 0	—	—
Ramsgate	—	—	17 0 0	34 6 0	5 5 0	3 0 0
Rochester	—	—	32 14 11	67 6 3	4 15 0	3 19 10
Sandwich	—	—	1 0 0	0 10 0	—	0 15 8
Sevenoaks	—	—	2 12 0	3 0 0	4 4 0	1 4 0
Sheerness	—	—	8 10 0	2 10 0	—	12 4 6
Shooter's Hill	—	—	0 1 6	—	—	—
Tenterden	—	—	0 12 6	0 10 0	—	0 6 6
Tonbridge	—	—	2 12 0	0 17 0	4 10 0	0 5 6
Tunbridge Wells	—	—	15 12 0	8 0 0	1 1 0	1 4 7
Wingham	—	—	1 0 0	0 5 0	—	—

Source: *Second Report from the Select Committee on Postage* (1838), Appendix E, No. 40, p. 179.

The majority of Kentish post towns appear to have been free from local delivery charges by 1784, but in some they lasted up to 1835. If such charges were abolished it meant the need for an immediate increase in the salary of the postmaster, as this source of revenue had been taken into account when his salary had been determined. The increase, when free delivery was introduced, was usually given in the form of a set sum in compensation each year, which ceased on the retirement of the postmaster then in office. As a consequence, where no complaints were received from the local inhabitants, private delivery charges were retained. This principle was clearly laid down by Francis Freeling in September 1828 following a complaint from an inhabitant of Sittingbourne. Writing to the Postmaster-General in regard to this case he stated:

> Your Grace is aware that the law officers have given an opinion that wherever we have an official Establishment we are bound to afford a free delivery of letters. This certainly entails considerable expense upon the Revenue, but where the gratuity is objected to, we have no alternative.

The last Kentish post towns to receive free delivery were Sevenoaks (April 1827), Cranbrook (December 1827), Sittingbourne (October 1828), Tonbridge (January 1829), Dartford (July 1829), Wingham (February 1834), and Tunbridge Wells (December 1835).[13] Tunbridge Wells was the last post town in the country to receive free delivery, and presented problems in arranging a free delivery area. In February 1830 when the question had been previously commented upon by Mr. Scott, the Surveyor, he had stated:

> Tunbridge Wells is however differently circumstanced to any other place with which I am acquainted. The houses are straggling and extend over a large space. It would be impossible to include all in a free delivery and yet it would be difficult to decide where to draw a line.

Despite this, free delivery was granted in December 1835 largely because of the complaints made by visitors unused to such delivery charges. The local populace, who had always paid, seemed by and large content to continue to do so. The post towns where free delivery was granted might find that the boundary of free delivery was drawn to include only the centre of the town. Especially in fast-expanding towns many of the inhabitants still had to pay for delivery. At Canterbury as late as December 1836 free delivery extended only to an area enclosed by the old city walls. Up to the early 1830s the Post Office seemed reluctant to extend the boundaries of post towns. In March 1831 an application for such an extension at Margate brought an admission that though when first established free delivery 'included the continuation of houses in every direction' the town had now 'greatly increased' in size. It was further stated that 'if long established delivery at Margate should be broken through, a similar concession must be expected at other watering places'.[14]

This attitude was soon to change. The boundaries of free delivery were increased at Dover (October 1836), Margate (November 1836), Canterbury (December 1836), Maidstone (July 1838), Ramsgate (January 1839), Sheerness (March 1839), and Tunbridge Wells (August 1839).[15] In the Rochester area even greater concessions were made. Before February 1835 all letters for Strood paid an additional ½d., letters between Rochester and Chatham paid 2d., and those from Chatham to New Brompton paid the same. At Gillingham the additional charge was 2d. for each letter delivered, and 1d. for each collected. Lord Maryborough, the Postmaster-General in 1835, ordered that the whole of this area was to be free of delivery charges in addition to general post rates, despite the considerable expense necessary to effect it. Two postmasters who tried to reimpose a form of local delivery charge after they had been removed were ordered to refrain from doing so.[16]

Even after free delivery had been universally adopted within post towns, the delivery of letters to areas beyond the boundary could be very lucrative for the postmasters. At both Dover and Gravesend the profits from this source were in 1838 more than their official salaries.[17] Apart from letters delivered to the outlying parts of the towns, postmasters were also entitled to any charge levied on letters put into the post for delivery to any other part of the same post town. At Margate in 1835 the total amounts collected on the delivery outside the free zone were £75 11s. 7d.; the postmaster's total delivery costs £14 4s. 0d. When the free area was extended the Post Office was obliged to meet in full the cost of the wages of the letter carriers (an additional £14 4s. 0d.) and also pay the postmaster £50 per annum in compensation for the extra halfpennies and pennies previously collected. Compensation of £60 per annum was paid to the Dover postmaster when free delivery was extended in this post town in the same year.[18]

An additional source of revenue for the Maidstone post-master was the income from participation in the post route from there to West Malling. The official post only operated three days a week to West Malling, and to Aylesford four days a week. On the other days the messenger was privately employed by the postmaster on the same route. Letters for West Malling were charged an extra 1d. on those days, and Aylesford and Larkfield an extra halfpenny. The charge applied both to letters delivered and those collected. No additional charge was made on the official post days. The postmaster paid the letter carrier £13 12s. 0d. in addition to his official salary of £16 per annum, and the receivers at Larkfield and Aylesford received an extra £1 6s. 0d. per annum from the postmaster. His profits from this post amounted to £60 per annum in 1816. In May 1836 it was proposed to make the post wholly official, but the idea was rejected as it would have meant increased cost in wages and compensation to the postmaster. Until May 1817 the Maidstone to Ashford route was served under a similar arrangement. This was an official three-day post, but mail was delivered on all six days, the postmaster paying the rider £45 15s. 0d. per annum extra, and charging a penny on every letter delivered to the inter-mediate villages. His profit was in the region of £50 per annum. A similar arrangement existed for the post route from Queen-borough through Minster, Eastchurch and Leysdown.[19]

Another source of revenue to postmasters were late posting fees. Letters handed in immediately prior to the departure of the mail paid an extra fee, usually 1d. or 2d. At Canterbury revenue from this source amounted to £31 1s. 5d. in 1837 and at Rochester £32 14s. 11d. At other offices amounts collected were much smaller, falling as low as 1s. 6d. in the case of Shooter's Hill. The charge was designed more to deter letters from being posted at times inconvenient to official office duties than as an extra source of revenue for the postmaster. At Tunbridge Wells in 1823 an extra penny was charged on letters posted after 8 pm., the London mail being due for departure at 8.30 pm. The fee was also a penny at Ramsgate in 1808, but this sum appears to have been sufficient to temp Sarah Hunt, 'a menial servant' left by the postmaster in charge of the office. She was accused of opening and reading three letters in her charge and putting 'the clock forward to obtain from persons bringing letters to the office the penny which is customary to receive for such as are after time'.[20]

Private boxes might bring the postmaster a small gratuity, but only two in Kent appear to have benefited in the year ending 5 January 1837. The Bromley postmaster had six subscribers from whom he received a guinea each, while his counterpart at Rochester had but one subscriber who paid eight pounds. The purpose of these boxes is explained as a footnote to a return in *The Second Report on Postage* (1838):

> Persons who have Private Boxes enjoy generally the advantage of receiving their letters as soon as the window is open and the Letter-carriers despatched, by which means, those Subscribers who reside at any distance from the office obtain their letters so much earlier than they would do by the ordinary Delivery; they have also the opportunity of ascertaining at once whether there are any letters for them, and are usually allowed credit by the Postmaster, accounts being kept of their Postage.

In October 1838 the Post Office laid down an official fee of two guineas for private firms and four guineas for public companies per annum, and henceforth fees were paid into the Post Office revenue.[21]

Profit for the sale of money orders was another perquisite. The Money Order Office was established in 1792 as a private venture controlled by the Clerks of the Roads, but in 1798 it came under new control. From this date it was run by three partners, the most important of whom was Daniel Stow, Superintendent President of the Inland Office. Most Kentish postmasters had an account with the Money Order Office, though a few of the small offices, and those near London, did not. One of the reasons put forward for the scheme when it was originally suggested was that it would enable sailors and soldiers to remit money home to their families. Certainly Chatham was in 1837 the office with the largest sale of money orders in the county, and Sheerness next in order. Only post-masters of post towns could have money order accounts, and facilities were refused at Whitstable in July 1828 as it was not a post town and only had a receiver.[22]

To offset salary and perquisites the postmaster had a number of expenses of which one of the heaviest was the need to provide an office at his own cost. In addition to this he had to provide out of his own pocket candles and coal, stationery, string and sealing wax. Although allowances were made by the Post Office for clerical assistance and letter carriers, these were often inadequate to meet the full cost. In 1837 the Chatham postmaster was paying £55 for a clerk whom he was employing out of his own pocket, and similar assistance was costing the Deal and Rochester postmasters £60 and £54 12s. 0d. respec-tively. The total expenses of the Rochester postmaster in April 1815 were £91 out of a total income of £173 8s. 0d. The office rent was £15, he employed a clerk at £30, though he had no allowance for one, and the letter carrier's wages were £31 4s. 0d. or £3 18s. 0d. more than the allowance given for him. Coal and candles cost £12, and wax and string £3.[23]

Below the deputy postmasters of post towns in status were sub-deputies. They appear to have been appointed at the larger villages on the general post routes and to have been responsible to the postmaster of the nearest post town. It was the postmaster who accounted for the letters and postage money collected, and who paid the sub-deputy his wages. The sub-deputies of both Goudhurst and Hawkhurst were under the control of the Lamberhurst postmaster. Wages were low. In July 1802 the Hawkhurst sub-deputy had his wages doubled from £3 to £6 per annum, and in 1817 they were raised to £10, eventually reaching £15 in 1838.[24] Even Tonbridge, a town of some size, was looked after by a sub-deputy until made a post town in its own right in July 1808. In 1838 sub-deputies existed at Biddenden (£5 per annum), Upper Walmer (£8 per annum), Rolvenden (£5 5s. 0d. per annum), Hawkhurst (£15 per annum), and Edenbridge (£3 3s. 0d. per annum).[25] Also appointed were receivers. This was the usual terminology for persons appointed on fifth clause and penny post routes. The primary function of these people, as their name suggests, was to receive letters from members of the public for collection by the letter carrier. The wages given were very low. In 1797 the receiver at Aylesford was granted only £1 1s. 0d. per annum, while £2 2s. 0d appears to have been a common rate of remuneration.[26] As late as January 1839 this was the sum given to the receiver at Godmersham. The receiver at Broadstairs had one of the largest salaries, in 1834 amounting to £20 per annum, but no salary at all had been given before May 1802, and gratuities on the delivery of letters was his sole source of revenue. Receivers accounted to the nearest post town for any money collected, and received their salary from the postmaster.[27]

Chapter 6

POST OFFICE SURVEYORS

THE GENERAL SUPERVISION of postal arrangements at local level was in the hands of the Post Office Surveyor for the district. In 1786 a system was introduced allowing for the appointment of six surveyors to be paid £100 per annum. and in addition a guinea for each day on the road. Kent was under the control of the Surveyor of the Home District whose area covered most of the Home Counties. Each surveyor was allowed a Post Office Mail Coach Guard to assist him in his duties.[1]

Surveyors were required to send in returns monthly of the performance of mail carts, riders and foot posts, detailing and explaining delays. The surveyor might also be required to report on certain specific post routes where it was thought that improvement of facilities was possible. Mr. Bartlett was ordered in January 1793, at the commencement of hostilities with France, to look into the Sittingbourne to Queensborough route which served the Sheerness naval base, and to investigate the possibility of an annual payment to the ferrymen for conveying 'the Mail across without any impediment' from the mainland to the Isle of Sheppey. When new routes were opened the surveyor had to check to see that they were functioning efficiently. Mr. Scott in November 1827 reported on the recently-opened Hastings to Dover route and the application of the postmaster of Hythe, as a consequence of this new post, for an evening delivery in the town. The surveyor was entirely responsible for the setting up of penny post routes down to the appointment of letter carriers and receivers.[2]

When deputies fell badly in arrears the surveyor might have to take charge of the office until another postmaster could be appointed. This occurred in June 1800 at Hythe and again at Tonbridge in February 1810. In the later case Mr. Aust, the surveyor, complained early in March that he had been at Tonbridge for 23 days and was fatigued by having to carry out night duties at the post office as well as conducting his normal duties during the day. On 4 April Mr. Aust was still at Tonbridge but a Mr. Gadby was sent to assist him 'that he might acquire some insight into the proceedings and begin to qualify himself to perform the duties of a surveyor'.[3]

The district surveyor was expected to instruct new post-masters on the nature of their duties, and stay with them until he was certain that their offices were functioning effi-ciently. This duty was at times delegated to others. In Kent Mr. Boorman, the postmaster of Lamberhurst, frequently deputised when the surveyor was dealing with matters else-where. The only other person who appears to have deputised for the surveyor in this way was the son of Mr. Hubbard, the Maidstone postmaster, who was employed in May 1827 to instruct the new postmaster of New Romney. The usual remuneration for such services was 15s. 0d. a day and coach fares, though in June 1817 for his work at Maidstone Mr. Boorman was paid 18s. 0d. a day and coach fare.[4]

District surveyors were also expected to look into com-plaints received from members of the public about postmasters or the postal service. Usually they conducted an on-the-spot enquiry and reported back to the Secretary of the Post Office in London. In November 1816 Dr. Hyde of Farnborough complained about the receiver, mentioning his neglect in the delivery of letters and general inattention to his duties. The surveyor found letters 'left loosely and carelessly about and the business of the office quite a secondary consideration', and he recommended the dismissal of the receiver. Accusa-tions made in December 1803 against the Sheerness postmaster included refusal to issue a money order to an old seaman of Greenwich Hospital, allowing unauthorised persons to sort the mail, detention of letters, drunkenness, and ill-treatment of his wife amongst others. The subsequent investigation led to his resignation in February 1804.[5]

———————

On 10 January 1840 the rate on prepaid letters weighing less than ½oz. was reduced to 1d., and on 6 May adhesive stamps came into use to enable letters to be prepaid more easily. These reforms associated with Rowland Hill had a considerable effect not only on the volume of mail but also on office procedures.[6] This, coupled with the use of the railway for the transmission of mail, resulted in great changes. The main line of the South Eastern Railway was open to Dover, and the branch to Maidstone completed by the year 1844. Next year came the Tunbridge Wells branch, and one year later that from Ashford to Margate via Canterbury. The mail coaches no longer ran. The new Post Office ceased to act as an agent of taxation, serving a minority of the populace and burdened with the free mail of a privileged few. It was now the servant of a much larger proportion of the British people, giving a more efficient service at its true cost.

APPENDIX 1

RISE IN KENTISH POSTAL REVENUE, 1673–79

(A) The Dover Road

Office	1673	1674	1675	1676	1677	1679	% increase period 1673–9
	Year ending 30 June						
	£ s. d.	£ s. d.	£ s. d.	£ s. d.	£ s. d.	£ s. d.	%
Dartford	12 15 8	17 13 1	17 2 2	19 2 9	21 3 0	31 0 5	142.6
Gravesend	—	34 15 0	25 6 1	26 6 8	30 15 2	45 16 8	31.8[2]
Rochester	223 15 7	201 12 11	140 8 0	142 11 11	138 6 0	157 8 1	–29.7[3]
Maidstone	61 6 7	61 7 10	63 10 1	62 19 8	67 8 4	92 3 2	50.3
Lenham	—	—	—	—	—	3 11 4	—[4]
Ashford	—	—	—	—	22 11 4	29 11 2	—
Sittingbourne	23 5 9	22 15 2	23 18 6	27 14 4	31 5 8	30 15 2	31.9
Queenborough	—	4 16 6	3 19 8	5 7 0	2 5 0[1]	—	—
Sheerness	—	—	—	—	—	11 0 6	—
Faversham	48 19 2	54 7 6	53 12 9	60 9 8	63 19 10	60 0 4	22.6
Canterbury	227 7 9	229 8 7	252 11 11	244 2 6	254 1 10	292 14 4	28.7
Dover	204 9 9	218 10 0	291 11 9	252 5 7	239 0 4	189 16 7	–12.5
Deal	66 11 7	99 13 10	93 5 10	108 12 9	115 8 0	159 8 4	139.5[5]
Sandwich	110 4 9	99 2 7	88 19 0	99 2 10	88 1 5	87 12 1	–20.6[6]
Margate	—	38 3 6	42 17 2	51 8 3	55 10 2	48 12 8	45.4[7]
Totals	978 16 7	1,082 6 6	1,097 2 11	1,100 3 11	1,129 16 1	1,239 10 10	26.6
% Rise	—	10.6%	1.4%	0.3%	2.4%	9.8%	—

Sources: P.O.R. Post 94 Peover Papers—Cash Books 1672–77; Post 3/1.

NOTES

1. July to November (only five months).
2. Percentage increase, 1674–8.
3. High figures for 1673 and 1674 probably a reflection of activity at Chatham Dockyard as a consequence of the Third Dutch War.
4. Up to 1677 all Ashford letters had been charged to the Maidstone postmaster as had also letters for Lenham before 1678. The increase for Maidstone is therefore probably higher than the 50.3 per cent. stated.
5. 1678 figure abnormally high, although reason for this is not clear.
6. Although the Sandwich postal revenue appears to be declining over this period, the 1673 figure is inflated as it included all Margate letters.
7. Percentage increase 1674–8.

APPENDIX 1—*continued.*

(B) The Rye Road

Office	1673 £ s. d.	Year ending 30 June 1674 £ s. d.	Year ending 30 June 1675 £ s. d.	1676 £ s. d.	1677 £ s. d.	1679 £ s. d.	% increase period 1673-9 %
Bromley	—	0 16 8	0 8 8	—	0 1 6	2 11 1	—
Chipstead	5 0 6	4 12 4	7 18 8	10 15 4^1	—	—	—
Sevenoaks	—	—	—	0 0 8^1	20 12 6	36 10 10	—
Tonbridge	8 16 1	10 4 11	16 8 11	25 9 8	55 17 9	68 12 4	679.5
Stonecrouch	1 11 0	2 15 9	5 3 9	7 14 0	9 15 10	11 15 0	658.1
Rye	28 5 4	34 1 0	35 19 4	41 7 11	48 5 5	40 16 8	44.4
Battle	—	—	—	—	4 8 8	4 19 1^2	—
Hastings	—	—	—	—	10 15 11	5 10 6^2	—
Totals	43 12 11	52 10 8	65 19 4	85 7 7	149 17 7	170 15 6	291.9
% Rise	—	20.4%	25.6%	29.4%	75.9%	13.9%	—

Source: P.O.R. Post 94, Peover Papers—Cash Books 1672-77.

NOTES

1. The Chipstead office was closed in June 1676, the Sevenoaks office opening as a replacement.
2. The figures for Battle and Hastings for the year 1679 represent only the six months July to December 1678.

APPENDIX 2

RISE IN KENTISH POSTAL REVENUE, 1678–1720

(A) The Dover Road

Office	1685[1]			Percentage increase on 1678/9 (2)	Year ending 25 Mar. 1721			Percentage increase on 1685 (3)
	£	s.	d.	%	£	s.	d.	%
Dartford	35	15	4	8.9	101	9	1	72,.
Gravesend	58	0	4	26.6	131	8	0	61.9
Rochester	189	18	8	17.1	263	7	0	—
Chatham	—			—	355	6	1	179.5[4]
Maidstone	132	7	0	43.6	337	9	9	106.3
West Malling	—			—	44	16	1	—
Ashford	59	15	6	102.2	159	13	4	90.8
Sittingbourne	32	14	8	6.2	85	17	10	87.4
Queenborough	—			—	98	18	11	—
Sheerness	20	7	0	84.6	—			245.6[6]
Faversham	68	11	0	14.3	121	1	0	26.2
Canterbury	303	0	0	3.9	508	17	5	19.9
Dover	163	17	2	−13.5	220	9	2	−3.9
Wingham	—			—	20	16	0	—
Deal	109	18	10	−37.2	249	15	3	63.0
Sandwich	92	19	2	6.1	131	16	2	1.3
Margate	44	8	2	−8.7	135	8	9	117.9
Folkestone	—			—	29	3	11	—
Hythe	—			—	25	10	6	—
New Romney	—			—	34	3	2	—
	1,311	12	10	5.6	3,055	7	5	66.7

APPENDIX 2—*continued.*

(B) **The Rye Road**

Office	1685[1]			Percentage increase on 1678/9 (2)	Year ending 25 Mar. 1721			Percentage increase on 1685 (3)
	£	s.	d.	%	£	s.	d.	%
Bromley	11	18	4	347.1	65	16	3	307.4
Sevenoaks	55	4	4	−19.4	193	4	7	150.0
Tonbridge	61	19	4	−9.7	243	16	0	181 0
Stonecrouch	15	7	4	−30.6	62	10	3	190.7
Rye	41	15	4	2.3	66	6	5	20.3
Cranbrook	—			—	62	9	4	—
Biddenden	—			—	18	8	0	—
Tenterden	—			—	43	11	0	—
Hurst Green	—			—	52	5	1	—
Battle	—			—	66	10	7	—
Hastings	—			—	51	0	4	—
	186	4	8	9.0	925	17	10	255.5[7]

Sources: P.O.R. Post 3/1, 3/6.

NOTES

1. Figures for the six months January to June only are recorded, the figures shown are these multiplied by two.

2. See Table at Appendix 1 on pp. 141–2.

3. Percentages adjusted to take into account a rise in postal rates in 1711, see p. 33.

4. Chatham letters previously charged on Rochester.

5. West Malling letters previously charged on Maidstone. The percentage of 106.3 per cent. increase shown for Maidstone is based on the inclusive revenue of both Maidstone and West Malling offices.

6. Office moved from Sheerness to Queenborough.

7. These figures show the effect of the ending of the farm of the offices of Cranbrook, Biddenden, Tenterden, Hurst Green, Battle and Hastings. The farm of Folkestone, Hythe and New Romney shown on the Dover Road Table, had also ceased. See pp. 49–50.

APPENDIX 3

KENTISH POSTAL REVENUE, 1720-1750

(A) The Dover Road

Office	1720[1] £	s.	d.	% increase or decrease	1730[2] £	s.	d.	% increase or decrease	1740[3] £	s.	d.	% increase or decrease	1750[4] £	s.	d.	% increase or decrease
				%				%				%				%
Dartford	101	9	1		101	11	3	0.1	108	1	3	12.6	111	13	8	3.3
Gravesend	131	8	0		108	11	10	−17.4	141	15	9	30.6	122	13	11	−13.4
Rochester	263	7	0		188	10	3	−28.4	244	3	1	29.3	253	16	6	6.7
Chatham	355	6	1		255	0	9	−36.7	330	11	2	27.6	300	14	4	−7.5
Maidstone	337	9	9		275	2	10	−18.5	317	5	2	29.3	289	19	8	−8.5
West Malling	44	16	1		47	16	3	6.8	48	10	9	1.6	50	17	10	4.9
Ashford	159	13	4		162	17	9	2.8	126	18	2	−28.4	125	3	7	−1.4
Sittingbourne	85	17	10		74	16	4	−13.0	105	15	2	41.4	82	8	2	−22.1
Queenborough	98	18	11		70	2	6	−28.7	90	4	9	28.5	92	17	1	2.9
Faversham	121	1	0		118	2	2	−2.4	126	14	9	7.3	111	10	9	−12.0
Canterbury	508	17	5		409	12	5	−19.5	449	7	6	9.9	475	1	0	5.7
Dover	220	9	2		216	17	8	−1.6	255	0	2	24.5	252	4	10	−1.1
Wingham	20	16	0		22	15	3	9.4	31	2	6	36.6	34	14	8	11.6
Deal	249	15	3		154	7	11	−37.9	178	15	5	16.0	147	13	1	−17.4
Sandwich	131	16	2		89	11	1	−32.1	149	14	0	67.7 }	283	14	4	−17.5
Margate	135	8	9		142	2	9	4.9	194	4	11	36.6				
Folkestone	29	3	11		30	8	9	4.1	32	9	11	6.7	34	11	2	6.0
Hythe	25	10	6		23	0	7	−9.8	32	14	7	42.3	33	0	7	0.9
New Romney	34	3	2		33	11	4	−1.8	33	6	0	−0.7	31	10	9	−5.3
Totals	3,055	7	5		2,524	19	8	−17.3	2,996	14	2	18.7	2,834	5	11	−5.4

APPENDIX 3—*continued.*

(B) The Rye Road

Office	1720[1]			% increase or decrease	1730[2]			% increase or decrease	1740[3]			% increase or decrease	1750[4]			% increase or decrease
	£	s.	d.	%	£	s.	d.	%	£	s.	d.	%	£	s.	d.	%
Bromley	65	16	3	6.0	69	15	1	6.3	74	3	6	31.9	97	16	9	31.9
Sevenoaks	193	4	7	−14.4	165	8	6	−7.0	153	15	4	3.7	159	9	0	3.7
Tonbridge	243	16	0	4.4	254	11	3	−26.1	184	13	10	5.9	195	11	9	5.9
Stonecrouch	62	10	3	−16.4	51	9	9	16.7	60	11	3	6.8	62	15	2	6.8
Rye	66	6	5	32.3	88	5	1	7.5	94	18	1	−4.5	90	12	0	−4.5
Cranbrook	62	9	4	−10.2	56	2	10	−10.3	50	6	7	−6.9	46	6	10	−6.9
Biddenden	18	8	0	−27.7	13	5	9	−15.8	11	4	3	−34.8	7	6	3	−34.8
Tenterden	43	11	0	−11.1	38	14	0	−13.6	33	8	9	−10.1	30	0	6	−10.1
Hurst Green	52	5	1	−20.4	41	11	9	8.4	45	1	3	−4.1	43	3	9	−4.1
Battle	66	10	7	−5.8	62	13	4	7.4	67	6	6	−6.0	65	5	3	−6.0
Hastings	51	0	4	−13.0	44	7	10	25.7	55	15	4	7.5	59	19	8	7.5
Totals	925	17	10	−4.4	886	5	2	−6.2	831	4	8	3.1	856	16	11	3.1

Sources: P.O.R. Post 3/6, Post 3/8, Post 3/10, Post 3/12.

NOTES

1. Year ending 25 March 1721.   2. Year ending 25 March 1731.
3. Year ending 25 March 1741.   4. Year ending 25 March 1751.

APPENDIX 4

COST OF RIDING WORK ON THE HASTINGS ROAD, 1791–1821

Date	Stage(s)	Distance (miles)	Total Contract Price (£ s. d.)	Price per double mile (£ s. d.)	Notes	References
1791	Southwark–Bromley	10	78 0 0	7 6 0	6d. a mile and 6d. for the driver each journey	Post 9/131
	Bromley–Sevenoaks	14	109 4 0	7 6 0		
	Sevenoaks–Tunbridge Wells	12	56 0 0	4 13 4		
	Tonbridge–Lamberhurst ..	10	46 13 4	4 13 4		
	Lamberhurst–Battle ..	16	74 13 4	4 13 4		
	Lamberhurst–Northiam	15	30 0 0	2 0 0	3 days only, on basis of six day week would equal £4 per double mile	
	Northiam–Rye... ..	8	16 0 0	2 0 0		
18 Aug. 1792	Sevenoaks–Tunbridge Wells ..	12	132 0 0	6 0 0	Increase back-dated to 10 Oct. 1790 when duty commenced	Post 42/59/1 Post 40/4/30
	Tonbridge–Lamberhurst ..	10				
24 June 1799	Sevenoaks–Lamberhurst ..	22		7 10 0	Addition of £25 to old rate for 12 months	Post 42/89/238; Post 40/61/81W
27 June 1799	London–Hastings ..	65	467 18 0	7 4 0		Post 42/89/244; Post 40/61/85N
27 Sept. 1804	London–Hastings and Rye ..	83			Extra allowance of £1 per mile till 5 April 1805	Post 42/96/114; Post 40/92/95S
	London–Hastings only ..	65	532 18 0	8 4 0		

APPENDIX 4–*continued.*

Date	Stage(s)	Distance	Total Contract Price			Price per double mile			Notes	References
			£	s.	d.	£	s.	d.		
21 Dec.	London–Lamberhurst	miles 46	467	10	6	10	3	3	6d. a mile for 7 days. In addition 32s. a week for 2 guards and £42 p.a. for keeping and repairing 2 covered carts. An increase of £111 12s. 6d. on old allowance. Contract for 12 months to 5 Jan. 1806 'under a penalty	Post 42/96/258; Post 40/93/59T
9 Nov.	London–Lamberhurst	46	498	5	6	10	16	8	£30 15s. 0d. increase to existing contractor to continue—no other person found to take on work at lower rates	Post 42/97/247; Post 40/100/33Y
12 June 1806	London–Lamberhurst	46	524	2	6	11	8	0	£56 12s. 0d. added to 21 Dec. 1804 rate as 'additional incidental allowance'	Post 42/98/51; Post 40/105/84A

APPENDIX 4–*continued*

Date	Stages(s)	Distance	Total Contract Price	Price per double mile	Notes	References
		miles	£ s. d.	£ s. d.		
24 June 1807	London–Lamberhurst	46	533 11 9	11 11 9		Post 42/99/175; Post 40/114/102E
21 Sept. 1807	London–Hastings	83	1,044 4 0	12 11 7	Exclusive of tax on horses and carts—£12 11s. 6d. per mile	Post 42/100/229; Post 40/125/76K
5 July 1809	London–Lamberhurst	46	600 0 0	13 0 1	Plus horse duties	Post 42/101/13 Post 42/101/24; Post 40/131/60N, Post 40/131/67N
30 Mar. 1810	London–Lamberhurst	46	550 0 0	11 19 2	Horse tax refunded in addition.	Post 42/101/397
	Lamberhurst–Hastings	37	511 11 0	13 16 6	This last year amounted to £44 9s. 2d.	
26 Feb. 1816	London–Lamberhurst	46	450 0 0	9 5 8	New contractor	Post 42/104/166; Post 42/104/195 Post 40/183/6, Post 40/184/50
1817	Lamberhurst–Hastings and Rye	37	400 0 0	10 16 3	New contractor	Post 42/104/471; Post 40/192/56

Replaced by mail coach 1821.

APPENDIX 5

LIST OF KENTISH FIFTH CLAUSE POSTS

Route	Date of commencement	Route (places in italics had receiving houses)	Remarks	Sources
1.—Maidstone to Tonbridge	1802	*Wateringbury, Mereworth, Hadlow*		P.O.R. Post 42/93/598
2.—Maidstone Area (circular route)	1802	*Tovil, East Farleigh, West Farleigh, Yalding, Hunton, Linton* (22 miles)	Walk deemed too long and divided—see 2A and 2B below	*Ibid.*
2A.—Maidstone Hunton	May 1807	*Tovil, East Farleigh, Barming, Teston, Yalding, Hunton* (10 miles)		P.O.R. 10A5, 10A8; Post 42/104/516, Post, 42/104/374, Post 42/105/348
2B.—Maidstone Staplehurst	May 1807	*Loose, Linton, Marden, Staplehurst* (9¼ miles)		P.O.R. 10A5, 10A8; Post 42/98/596, Post 42/113/219, Post 42/136/208, Post 42/136/306
3.—Lamberhurst to Goudhurst	1802	*Goudhurst*, extended in 1813 to *Horsemonden*	Converted to a penny post April 1837	P.O.R. 10A8; Post 9/132; Post 30 Pt. II/908X (1837); Post 42/93/278

APPENDIX 5 *—continued.*

Route	Date of commencement	Route (places in italics had receiving house)	Remarks	Sources
4.—Dartford to Sevenoaks	July 1804	*Sutton-at-Home, Farningham,* Enysford, Lullingstone, *Shoreham,* Otford, *Kemsing,* Seal, Igtham, *Wrotham*	Two messengers—one starting from Dartford, the other from Sevenoaks. Changed bags at Kemsing (later Otford). Route from Sevenoaks operated as penny post from Dec. 1827	P.O.R. Post 9/132; Post 35/28/233; Post 42/95/604, Post 42/129/337
5.—Dartford to Erith	Sept. 1802	*Crayford, Bexley,* North Cray, *Erith*	June 1825—Receiving house set up at *Bexley Heath* with an auxiliary messenger *Bexley* to Welling. Converted to penny post Feb. 1839	P.O.R. Post 35/20/147; Post 42/93/581, Post 42/105/398, Post 42/110/323, Post 42/112/49
6.—Chislehurst to Chelsfield	Sept. 1802	Sidcup, *Footscray,* St. Paul's Cray, *St. Mary's Cray, Orpington, Chelsfield*		P.O.R. Post 9/132; Post 35/30/147; Post 42/93/581
7.—Tunbridge Wells to East Grinstead	Sept. 1805	*Langton Green, Groombridge, Withyham, Hartfield, Forest Row*	Converted to a penny post July 1823	P.O.R. 10A13; Post 42/97/112

APPENDIX 6

LIST OF KENTISH PENNY POSTS

Post Town Responsible	Route and location of Receiving Houses	Mode of Conveyance	Date Established[1]	Remarks	Sources[2]
Ashford	1.–Willesborough, Mersham, Smeeth, Brabourne Lees	Foot Messenger	December 1816	Originally a military post to an army camp at Brabourne Lees	P.O.R. Post 42/104/406
	2.–Wye	Foot messenger	December 1816		P.O.R. Post 42/104/409
Bromley	Hayes, Hayes Common	Auxiliary foot messenger	14 Feb. 1833		
Canterbury	1.–Blean, Whitstable, Whitstable Road	Foot Messenger	October 1823		P.O.R. Post 42/110/118
	2.–Chartham, Chilham, Godmersham	Foot messenger	January 1839		P.O.R. Post 35/29/203
	3.–Bridge, Kingston, Barham, Half-Way House	Foot messenger	1 August 1824		P.O.R. Post 42/111/82
	Barham to Elham	Auxiliary foot messenger			
	4.–Sturry, Herne Street, Herne Bay	Horse post	March 1832		P.O.R. Post 42/127/468

APPENDIX 6–*continued.*

Post Town Responsible	Route and location of Receiving Houses	Mode of Conveyance	Date Established[1]	Remarks	Sources[2]
Cranbrook	Beneden, Smarden	Foot messenger	June 1839		P.O.R. Post 35/30/573
Dartford	1.–Greenhithe, Stone, Swanscombe	Foot messenger	November 1830		P.O.R. Post 42/124/326
	2.–Bexley	Foot messenger	February 1839	Previously a Fifth Clause Post	P.O.R. Post 35/31/241
Deal	Walmer Road, Walmer	Foot messenger	February 1822		P.O.R. Post 42/108/50, Post 42/109/318
Dover	Buckland, River, Ewell	Foot messenger	11 June 1824		P.O.R. Post 42/110/563
Faversham	Selling, Boughton Under Blean	Foot messenger	April 1824		P.O.R. Post 42/110/420
Folkestone	Sandgate	Dover to New Romney General Post rider	August 1814		P.O.R. Post 42/103/524

APPENDIX 6—*continued.*

Post Town Responsible	Route and location of Receiving Houses	Mode of Conveyance	Date Established[1]	Remarks	Sources[2]
Gravesend	Northfleet	Foot messenger	July 1814	Twice daily	P.O.R. Post 42/103/494
Hythe	Dymchurch	Foot messenger			
Lamberhurst	Goudhurst, Horsemonden, Brenchley	Foot messenger	April 1837	Previously a Fifth Clause Post	P.O.R. Post 30/Pt. II/ 908X (1837)
Maidstone	1.—Berstead, Park Gate, Sandway, Harrietsham, Lenham, Charing, Hoathfield	Maidstone to Ashford General Post rider	May 1817	Previously served by a general post route and private arrangements made by the Maidstone postmaster	P.O.R. Post 42/104/516
	2.—Otham, Langley, Sutton Valence, Headcorn	Foot messenger	July 1816	Extension to Headcorn from Sutton Valence, September 1834	P.O.R. Post 42/104/608, Post 42/133/517
Margate	1.—Broadstairs, Ramsgate	Ramsgate to Margate foot post	29 September 1834	See also Ramsgate	
	2.—Birchington, Sarre	Foot messenger	1838		

APPENDIX 6—*continued.*

Post Town Responsible	Route and location of Receiving Houses	Mode of Conveyance	Date Established [1]	Remarks	Sources [2]
New Romney	1.—Lydd	Foot messenger	22 February 1834	Delivered twice daily	P.O.R. Post 42/132/315
	2.—Brookland	Delivered by Hastings to Dover mail cart	18 February 1833		
Ramsgate	Broadstairs, St. Peters	Ramsgate to Margate foot post	June 1827	From 29 September 1834 extended to Margate. 2d. charged Margate to Ramsgate. St. Peters to R.H. estb. 6 June 1835	P.O.R. Post 42/133/534
Sevenoaks	1.—Halstead		March 1839		P.O.R. Post 35/29/233
	2.—Kemsing, Seal, Igtham, Wrotham	Foot messenger	December 1827	Replacement for part of the Sevenoaks to Dartford Fifth Clause Post	P.O.R. Post 35/29/233 P.O.R. Post 42/115/210
	Otford, Shoreham (from Wrotham)	Auxiliary foot messenger			
	3.—Riverhead, Chipstead, Chart, Sundridge, Brasted, Westerham		March 1810		P.O.R. Post 42/100/616 Post 42/101/398
	Edenbridge (from Westerham)	Foot messenger	March 1839		P.O.R. Post 35/29/233

APPENDIX 6—*continued.*

Post Town Responsible	Route and location of Receiving Houses	Mode of Conveyance	Date Established[1]	Remarks	Sources[2]
Shooter's Hill	Woolwich, Plumstead, Eltham, Lewisham, Blackheath, Greenwich, Lee, Old Charlton, New Charlton, Deptford	Carried by London District Post Messengers	6 March 1835	Established to prevent the need to take letters for S.E. London to the G.P.O. first	P.O.R. Post 42/136/31
Sittingbourne	1.—Green Street, Linstead, Newnham, Doddington	Foot messenger	September 1814		P.O.R. Post 42/103/531
	2.—Key Street, Newington, Rainham	Foot messenger	June 1815		P.O.R. Post 42/104/47
Tonbridge	1.—Pembury	Foot messenger	21 September, 1834		P.O.R. Post 42/133/475
Tunbridge Wells	Langton Green, Groombridge, Withyham, Hartfield, Forest Row (to East Grinstead)	Foot messenger	Existed by 1823	Previously a Fifth Clause Post	
Wingham	Ash	By Deal	October 1836	Bag made up at Wingham and forwarded to the Receiver by the Deal coach. The Receiver delivered in the village	P.O.R. Post 42/138/266

NOTES

1. Where the date of opening is not known the date quoted is that of the Surveyor's report recommending the commencement of the service.
2. Apart from the sources indicated in this column the following were used: P.O.R. 10A8, 10A13; Post 9/132; *First Report from the Select Committee on Postage* (1838), Appendix 24, pp. 474f.

APPENDIX 7

MAIN POST ROUTES AND THEIR IMPROVEMENTS, 1784-1840

From	To	Main Changes	Date	Sources
London	Dover	1.—Coach re-routed to call at Chatham. 2.—Coach no longer passed through Faversham. Foot messenger collected mail from the coach on the main road and brought it into the town.	April 1821 April 1834	P.O.R. Post 42/107/288 P.O.R. Post 42/132/484
Rochester	Maidstone	Mail taken from Maidstone to Key Street instead of Rochester to connect with the London coach. Found to be unsatisfactory and old routing via Rochester restored by 1838.	1830	P.O.R. Post 42/123/255, Post 42/123/337; *3rd Rep. from the Select Committee on Postage* (1838), postal distribution map
Maidstone	West Malling	1.—Official 3-day post in 1784. Official 4-day post to Aylesford and new receiving house at Larkfield. 2.—A route from Larkfield to East Malling is shown on a postal distribution map of 1813. No other reference.		P.O.R. Post 42/68/250, Post 42/68/367 P.O.R. 10A8
Maidstone	Ashford	Three-day official post in 1784 made an official daily post. Intermediate villages served by a penny post.	May 1817	P.O.R. Post 42/104/516
Ashford	Canterbury	New post established.	August 1830	P.O.R. Post 42/124/62
Sitting-bourne	Queenborough	1.—Sheerness made a post town and route extended from Queenborough	June 1799	P.O.R. Post 42/72/400, Post 42/89/97, Post 42/89/253

APPENDIX 7 —*continued.*

From	To	Main Changes	Date	Sources
—*continued*—		2.—Two-day official post from Queenborough to Minster, Eastchurch and Leysdown. By 1838 on official 3-day post.	Date of establishment not known but in existence in 1824	P.O.R. Post 42/111/200; Post 9/132; 10A8, 10A13
Canterbury	Deal	Mail coaches used as early as 1792, but in regular use from 1823.		P.O.R. Post 42/103/12
Sandwich	Margate	1.—Route diverted to serve Broadstairs. 2.—Replaced by a direct Canterbury to Margate and Canterbury to Ramsgate routes operated in the summer months by coaches.	October 1790 Coaches already on this route in the summer by 1793	P.O.R. Post 9/131 P.O.R. Post 42/72/34
Deal	Dover	New horse post.	May 1835	P.O.R. Post 42/135/451
Dover	New Romney	1.—Made a daily post, previously only four days. 2.—Extended to Hastings.	August 1792 Nov. 1827	P.O.R. Post 42/59/53 P.O.R. Post 42/117/160
Bromley	Farnborough	Set up to save Hastings mail from having to stop at Farnborough. Carried by coach at first but from c. 1817 this method of conveyance discontinued.	April 1809	P.O.R. Post 42/100/591, Post 42/104/446
Lamberhurst	Rye	Daily post served by mail cart. Previously only a 3-day post.	1794	P.O.R. Post 42/40/78

APPENDIX 7 *—continued.*

From	To	Main Changes	Date	Sources
Lamberhurst	Tenterden	1.—Changed to two posts (a) ride from Hawkhurst to Tenterden. (b) footpost from Forsters Green to Biddenden. Both posts previously 3-day posts.	1802	P.O.R. Post 43/93/278
		2.—Ride Hawkhurst to Tenterden discontinued and re-placed to two footposts: (a) Hawkhurst–Cranbrook–Biddenden. (b) Newenden–Rolvenden–Tenterden.	1811	P.O.R. Post 42/102/415, Post 42/102/441; Post 35/111/229
London	Hastings	1.—Mail coach routed via Tunbridge Wells.	Feb. 1824 –June 1827	P.O.R. Post 42/110/364, Post 42/116/196, Post 42/132/519
		2.—Foot messenger used Tonbridge to Tunbridge Wells.	June 1827 –April 1834	
		3.—Mail coach re-routed via Tunbridge Wells again, but did not call at post office. Mail conveyed from Calverley Road to post office by a foot post.	April 1834	
Maidstone	Staplehurst	1.—Extended to Cranbrook and changed from a foot to a horse post.	July 1835	P.O.R. Post 42/136/208; *3rd Rep. from the Select Committee on Postage* (1838), postal distribution map
		2.—Further extended to Hawkhurst.	1838	
Battle	Lewes	Replaced by a route from Tunbridge Wells to Lewes.	1839	P.O.R. Post 35/31/573

REFERENCES

Chapter 1

1. Howard Robinson, *The British Post Office—A History* (Princeton 1948), pp. 1–29.

2. *H.M.C. 12th Report*, Appendix Pt. 1, p. 478; P.R.O. SP/16/231.

3. P.R.O. SP/16/231.

4. *H.M.C. 12th Report*, Appendix Pt. II, p. 6.

5. *Ibid.*

6. *Ibid.*, p. 37.

7. The actual agreement was signed between Thomas Witherings and M. Deonveau at Calais and dated 11 May 1636. It was issued as a royal proclamation in England under the title, *A Proclamation concerning the carrying and recarrying of Letters as well within his Majesties Realmes and Dominions as into and from foreigne parts.*

8. P.R.O. SP16/307.

9. *Cal. S.P. (Dom.)* 1635, p. 166, transcript in W. G. Stitt-Dibden (ed.), *The British Post Office 1635-72* (Bath 1960), p. 7.

10. *Cal. S.P. (Dom.)* 1635, p. 166; Stitt-Dibden, *op. cit.*, p. 6.

11. *Cal. S.P. (Dom.)* 1635, p. 29; Stitt-Dibden, *op. cit.*, p.7.

12. Stitt-Dibden, *op. cit.*, p. 8.

13. Robinson, *op. cit.*, p. 35.

14. *Cal. S.P. (Dom.)*, 1635-6, pp. 31, 1636-7, p. 225, 1637, p. 331.

15. *H.M.C. 12th Report*, Appendix Pt. II, p. 171.

16. *Cal. S.P. (Dom.)* 1636-7, p. 225.

17. *Ibid.*, 1633, pp. 56, 69.

18. *Ibid.*, 1649-50, p. 439; *H.M.C. 12th Report*, Appendix Pt. II, p. 84; John Taylor, *The Carriers Cosmograpnie* (1637); Robinson, *op. cit.*, p. 33.

19. K.C.A.O. Sa/C4/25.

20. *Cal. S.P. (Dom.)* 1636-6, p. 31; *H.M.C. 12th Report*, Appendix Pt. II, p. 159.

21. *Cal. S.P. (Dom.)* 1640-1, p. 39.

22. Robinson, *op. cit.* pp, 33, 37.

23. *Cal. S.P. (Dom.)* 1640-1, p. 475, 1641-3. pp. 283, 501.

24. A. M. Everitt, *The Community of Kent and the Great Rebellion 1640-60* (Leicester 1966), p. 165.

25. Joan Parkes, *Travel in England in the Seventeenth Century* (1925), p. 122; John Evelyn, *The Diary of John Evelyn* (Oxford Standard Authors Series) (1959), p. 291.

26. *Cal. S.P. (Dom.)* 1649-50, p. 535, 1650, p. 7, 1654, p. 407; C. H. Firth and R. S. Rait (ed.) *Acts and Ordinances of the Interregnum* (1911), Vol. II, pp. 1110-3.

27. *Cal. S.P. (Dom.)* 1656-7, p. 82, 1657-8. p. 3.

28. K.C.A.O. Sa/C4/14, 25, 26; Everitt, *op. cit.*, p. 287; *Cal. S.P. (Dom.)* 1649-50, p. 439.

29. *Cal. S.P. (Dom.)* 1651-2, p. 543, 1652-3, p. 311.

30. *An Ordinance Touching the Office of Postage of Letters, Inland and Foreign*, 2 Sept. 1654. Transcript in Stitt-Dibden, *op. cit.*, p. 15; B.M. Add MSS. 22546/109.

31. *Orders by the Protector for the Postal Service in England, Scotland and Ireland. Cal. S.P. (Dom.)* 1655, p. 285.

Chapter 2

1. Howard Robinson, *The British Post Office—A History* (Princeton 1948), pp. 49-50; Howard Robinson, *Britain's Post Office* (1953), Appendix II, p. 283.

2. See p. 55.

3. J. C. Hemmeon, *The History of the British Post Office* (Harvard, 1912), pp. 243-4.

4. See Appendix 1, pp. 141-2.

5. See Appendices 2 and 3, pp. 143-6.

6. See pp. 49-50.

7. See Appendix 3, pp. 145-6.

8. Phyllis Deane and W. A. Cole, *British Economic Growth 1688-1959* (2nd edn, 1967), p. 103.

9. See p. 14.

10. See Appendix 3, pp. 145-6.

11. Hemmeon, *op. cit.*, p. 243-4.

12. Includes Sussex offices on the Rye/Hastings Road, i.e., Hurst Green, Battle, Hastings, and Rye.

13. See pp. 20-7.

14. See pp. 49-50.

15. P.O.R. Post 1/12/297; Post 14/1/36, 42.

16. P.R.O. SP29/218/84-88. See pp. 7-8 for an instance of the use of 'cuntry' or computed miles as opposed to 'post' or measured miles.

17. P.R.O. SP29/363/177; P.O.R. Post 94/11; B. M. Harleian MS. 7365 (Transcript in Thomas Gardiner, *A General Survey of the Post Office 1677-82*, ed. Foster W. Bond [Bath 1958]); G. F. Gent, *The Secretary's Guide* (1759); John Playfair, *Vade Mecum, or the Necessary Companion* (1679).

18. P.O.R. Post 14/1/45; B. M. Harleian MS. 7365; W. G. Stitt-Dibden (ed.) *The British Post Office 1635-62* (Bath 1960), pp. 25-9; Thomas Delawne, *The Present State of England* (1681), pp. 245--6; Strype's edition of Stowe's *Survey of London* (1720); *St. Martin-le-Grand Magazine*, Vol. 5 (1895).

19. See p. 12.

20. John Evelyn, *The Diary of John Evelyn* (Oxford Standard Authors) (1959). Evelyn used this route on his return from France in 1641 (p. 43), and 1652 (p. 315), and on his journeys to France in 1649 (p. 279), and 1650 (p. 291); Joan Parkes, *Travel in England in the Seventeenth Century* (1925), p. 57; Daniel Defoe, *A Tour Through England and Wales* (1724-6) Everyman edn., Vol. 1, p. 101.

21. P.O.R. Post 94/12/445, Post 94/16/411.

22. P.R.O. SP29/218, SP29/263/124; Frank Staff, *The Penny Post 1680-1918* (1964), p. 28.

23. P.O.R. Post 91/14/339, 426, 429, 452.

24. P.R.O. SP29/263/124; P.O.R. Post 94/12/445, Post 94/14/600, 606, 644, Post 94/16/313.

25. P.O.R. Post 42/68/250.

26. P.O.R. Post 3/10; Defoe, *op, cit.*, p. 105.

27. Defoe, *op. cit.*, pp. 109–110.

28. P.O.R. Post 3/5; Post 94/12/495, Post 94/16/490-1.

29. P.O.R. Post 94/12/290, 371, Post 94/16/286.

30. P.R.O. SP29/218; B.M. G6463 (Grenville Library); K.C.A.O. Sa/C4/25, Sa/C4/26.

31. P.O.R. Post 3/3; Post 94/16/128, 226; Defoe, *op. cit.*, pp. 119–120.

32. *Cal. T.B.*, Vol. XX, Pt. I, p. ccxxi, Vol. XXV, p. cdxviii, Vol. XXVII, p. ccclxxx.

33. Anon., *A Plan for the Better Regulation of the Footscray Post* (1768).

34. Celia Fiennes, *The Journey of Celia Fiennes*, ed. Christopher Morris (1949), p. 126; John Ogilby, *Britannia* (1675), p. 35.

35. 26 Geo. II cap. 68.

36. J. H. Andrews, 'Rye Harbour in the Reign of Charles II', *Sussex Archaeological Collections*, Vol. XCIV (Lewes 1956), pp. 35–42; Celia Fiennes, *op. cit.*, p. 138.

37. A hamlet 1½ miles N.W. of Flimwell and just inside the present Kent county border (TQ 700332).

38. P.R.O. SP29/179/21(i), SP29/218, SP29/263/124.

39. P.O.R. Post 94/12/468, 471, Post 94/14/666, 668, 675, Post 94/16/160, Post 94/11; Post 3/1; Thomas Gardiner, *op. cit.*, pp. 62. 68.

40. P.O.R. Post 94/11, Post 94/12/227.

41. Celia Fiennes, *op. cit.*, pp. 133–6; Defoe, *op. cit.*, p. 127.

42. E.S.C.R.O. Sayer MS. 1450B; *London Gazette*, 4–7 July 1687, 18–22 June 1728; *Court and City Register*, No. 6684 (1753); *Court and City Kalender* (1765).

43. P.O.R. Post 3/6, 3/8, 3/10, 3/11, 3/12; *Cal. T.B.*, Vol. XX, Pt. I, p. cccxxi.

44. Ogilby, *op. cit.*, p. 61; 8 Anne cap. 12.

45. 22 Geo. II cap. 4, 14 Geo. II cap. 12, 26 Geo. II cap. 54.

46. Quoted in Thomas Burke, *Travel in England* (1942), p. 71f.

47. E.S.C.R.O. Sayer MS. 1450B.

48. 2 Geo. III cap. 72.

49. Ogilby, *op. cit.*, *passim*; Celia Fiennes, *op. cit.*, p. 136.

50. Thomas Delawne, *The Present State of London* (1681), p. 346.

51. P.O.R. Post 94/14/103, Post 94/16/63, 219, 416.

52. P.O.R. Post 94/12/217, Post 94/14/30, Post 94/16/415; B.M. Harleian MS. 7365.

53. P.O.R. Post 94/12/30, 106, 144, Post 94/14/52, 187, 246, 796, Post 94/16/63, 312, 314; Howard Robinson, *The British Post Office—A History* (Princeton 1948), pp. 59-60.

54. P.O.R. Post 94/14/246, 410, 472.

55. P.R.O. SP29/226, Jan.-Mar. 1667, SP29/227, Apr.-May 1667, and SP29/228 May-Aug. 1667 are a miscellaneous collection of post labels covering all post roads with very few from the Dover Road. SP29/252 covering the period Feb.-Aug. 1668 is a collection of a further 65 post labels most of which refer to the Dover Road.

56. Ogilby, *op. cit.*, p. 35.

57. J. C. Hemmeon, *op. cit.*, p. 100f, lists journey times between London and Dover as from 19 to 22 hours. His conclusions appear to be based entirely on *Cal. SP. (Dom.)*, 1666-7, pp. 388-9, where only two journeys are in fact listed, one taking 19 hours and the other 22 hours. Although he lists *Cal. SP. (Dom.)*, 1667-8, pp. 116-21, as one of his references he clearly did not use it to reach his conclusions as several journey times of 18 hours are listed, and one of as little as 15 hours.

58. P.R.O. SP29/226, SP29/227, SP29/228, SP29/252.

59. 12 Car. II cap. 35.

60. 9 Anne cap 10.

61. 5 Geo. III cap. 25.

62. An average percentage increase in postal rates of 40 per cent. has been assumed in calculating the percentage rise in revenue at each office during the period 1685-1721 in Appendix 2, pp. 143-4. It is likely that the majority of the letters posted in Kent would be for London and would fall into the class of letters travelling less than 80 miles.

63. B. R. Mitchell and Phyllis Deane, *Abstract of British Historical Statistics* (1962), p. 468. According to the Schumpter-Gilboy price indices, starting from a base level of 100 in 1701, the index figure for consumer goods had reached 135 in 1711. It fell, however, to 101 in the following year, and from then to 1770 was only above 100 in 13 out of the 57 years.

64. P.O.R. Post 94/12/203, Post 94/16/136.

65. P.O.R. Post 94/12/100, 134, Post 94/14/159, Post 94/16/346.

66. P.O.R. Post 94/14/122, 294, Post 94/16/286; B.M. Harleian MS. 7365.

67. P.O.R. Post 94/14/727, Post 94/16/85, 88, 261, 299; Post 94/20/31.

68. P.O.R. Post 94/12/226, Post 94/14/632, 686, Post 94/16/107, 112, 140, 263.

69. P.O.R. Post 94/12/224, Post 94/14/246, 413, 467, Post 94/16/1, 27, 441, Post 94/20/31.

70. P.O.R. Post 94/12/338, 458, Post 94/14/443, 520, Post 94/16/112, Post 94/20/31.

71. P.O.R. Post 94/12/404, Post 94/14/217, 223, 226, Post 94/16/226, 255, 280, 281, Post 94/20/31; Parkes, *op. cit.*, p. 158.

72. *St. James's Chronicle* 1478, 11-14 Aug. 1770, 1663, 19-22 Oct. 1771, 1665 24-26 Oct. 1771, 1669 2-5 Nov. 1771, 1683 5-7 Dec. 1771; *The Public Advertiser* 14413, 19 Dec. 1780; *The London Courant*, 12 Feb. 1782; John Barrows, *Knights of the High Toby* (1962), pp. 234-255.

72. P.O.R. Post 94/20/30, 31, Post 94/14/242, *Cal. S.P. (Dom.).* 1666-7, p. 415.
74. *Cal. T.B. and P.*, Vol. IV, p. 803, Vol. VI, p. 51.

Chapter 3

1. P.O.R. SP29/74, SP29/112/121; *Cal. S.P. (Dom.)*, 1660-1, pp. 46, 97, 99, 1668-9, p. 135.
2. P.O.R. Post 1/5/162; Post 94/12/438; *Cal. S.P. (Dom.)*, 1659-60, p. 387, 1660-1, pp. 97, 99, 1672-3, p. 417.
3. P.O.R. Post 94/12/224, Post 94/14/337, 425, 606, Post 94/16/128.
4. P.O.R. Post 94/12/164, 202, Post 94/14/606, Post 94/16/232, 332.
5. P.O.R. Post 1/1/73, Post 94/12/426, 442, 448, Post 94/14/47, 410; Post 1/3/162.
6. P.O.R. Post 3/3, 3/4, 3/5, 3/6, 3/7, 3/8, 3/9; Post 94/1, 94/2, 94/3, 94/4, 94/5; B.M. Harleian MS 7365.
7. Wages rates and prices were also tending to rise generally from the end of the Seven Years War. See Mitchell and Deane, *op. cit.*, pp. 347, 469.
8. P.O.R. Post 94/14/192, 249, 267, 287, 289, 509, 562, Post 94/16/124, 266.
9. P.O.R. Post 94/12/426, Post 94/14/464, 480, 483, 749, Post 94/16/57; *Cal. S.P. (Dom.)*, 1667, p. 80.
10. P.O.R. Post 94/12/144, Post 94/16/3, 23, Post 94/16/299; Delawne, *op. cit.*, p. 346; *H.M.C.*, Appendix to Seventh Report.
11. James Presnail, *Chatham—The Story of a Dockyard Town and the Birthplace of the British Navy* (Chatham 1952), p. 116-7.
12. Quoted in Howard Robinson, *The British Post Office—A History* (Princeton 1948), pp. 67-9.
13. P.O.R. Post 94/14/350, Post 94/16/208; *Cal. S.P. (Dom.)*, 1671-2, p. 57; *St. James's Evening Post*, No. 5818.
14. Letters between places on the same post road and therefore not passing through the General Letter Office in London.
15. B.M. Harleian MS. 7365.
16. P.O.R. Post 94/12/393. The farm was to exclude the section of the Rye Road from London to Chipstead, the first stage, though it is difficult to understand why this section should have been retained by the Post Office.
17. P.O.R. Post 3/3, 3/4; Post 94/1, 94/2, 94/2, 94/4, 94/5; *Cal. T.B.*, Vol. XX, Pt. I, p. ccxxi, Vol. XXI, Pt. I, p. cccix, Vol. XXVI, Pt. I, p. cclxvii.
18. *Ibid.*, P.O.R. Post 94/16/413; Celia Fiennes, *op. cit.*, p. 134.
19. P.O.R. Post 94/12/217, Post 94/14/324, 659, 668, 673; *Cal. S.P. (Dom.)*, 1668-9, p. 295; Anon., *A Plan for the Better Regulation of the Footscray Post* (1768).
20. P.O.R. Post 1/10/15, Post 1/10/90; Post 94/12/322, Post 94/16/203.
21. B.M. Harleian MS. 7365; P.O.R. Post 94/12/321, Post 94/14/352, 400, Post 94/16/43, 69.

22. P.O.R. Post 94/12/202, 307, 338.

23. P.O.R. Post 94/11, Post 94/12/445, Post 94/14/260, 266, 274, 276; Gardiner, *op. cit.*, p. 16.

24. B.M. Harleian MS. 7365; P.O.R. Post 1/4/71; Stitt-Dibden, *op. cit.*, p. 26.

25. P.O.R. Post 94/14/275, 664, Post 94/16/1, 232, 314, 416.

26. P.O.R. Post 94/14/424, 430, 437.

27. P.O.R. Post 94/12/400, 403, 413, Post 94/14/339, 644, Post 94/16/1-; K.C.A.O. Sa/C4/26.

28. P.O.R. Post 94/14/386, Post 94/16/140; C. W. Chalklin, *Seventeenth Century Kent* (1965), p. 171; Defoe, *op. cit.*, pp. 112-3, 119.

29. P.O.R. Post 94/14/51, 60, 103, 132, 187, 249, 287, 313, 401, 563, 601, 633; P.O.R. Post 94/16/1, 63, 106; P.R.O. SP29/219/120; Stitt-Dibden, *op. cit.*, p. 28; *Cal. S.P. (Dom.)*, 1667, pp. 518, 519, 1670, p. 632.

Chapter 4

1. See pp. 49-50.

2. Howard Robinson, *The British Post Office—A History* (Princeton 1948), pp. 101ff.

3. See pp. 100-114.

4. J. C. Henmeon, *The History of the British Post Office* (Harvard 1912), pp. 243-6;

5. See pp. 90, 92-4.

6. P.O.R. Post 3/19, 3/24, 3/25; Henmeon, *op. cit.*, pp. 243-6; Howard Robinson, *Britain's Post Offices* (1953), Appendix II, p. 283; see pp. 90, 92-4 for the effect of population on postal services in Kent.

7. P.O.R. Post 1/12/297; Henmeon, *op. cit.*, pp. 243-6;

8. P.O.R. Post 3/20, 3/21, 3/24, 3/25; *First Report from the Select Committee on Postage* (1838), pp. 435, 444.

9. See pp. 58-9.

10. See pp. 63-4, 157-9.

11. See pp. 70-83.

12. See pp. 86-9.

13. See pp. 90, 92-4.

14. See pp. 89-91.

15. See Table V, p. 62.

16. See pp. 94-100.

17. See pp. 127, 132-3.

18. See pp. 79-80, 147-9.

19. See pp. 100-114, 150-6.

20. See pp. 157-9.

21. See pp. 100-114, 150-6.

22. See pp. 64, 67, 70-6.

23. P.O.R. Post 40/11/198A, Post 40/65/63Y; Post 42/62/99, Post 42/90/56; William Cobbett, *Rural Rides* (Penguin English Library Edn., 1967), p. 210.

24. P.O.R. Post 10/24/18; Post 40/9/25A, Post 40/65/81Y; Post 42/61/119, Post 42/90/83.

25. 41 Geo. III cap. 89.

26. P.O.R. Post 40/125/76K, Post 40/141/15S; Post 42/100/299, Post 42/101/562; H.L.R.O. Minutes of Evidence H.C., 1836, Vol. 36, South-Eastern Railway, 24 March, p. 245.

27. H.L.R.O. Minutes of Evidence H.C., 1836, Vol. 36, South-Eastern Railway, 23 March, pp. 249, 259, 24 March, pp. 17–21, 137, 245, 25 March, pp. 91, 93.

28. P.O.R. Post 40/60/110V, Post 40/65/81Y; Post 42/89/27, Post 42/90/83.

29. P.O.R. Post 30/474X (1814); Post 40/233/141; Post 42/107/288, Post 42/132/484; *The General Evening Post*, No. 8140, 5–7 Jan. 1786; *The London Chronicle*, No. 4555, 26–28 June 1786.

30. P.O.R. Post 9/131, pp. 2–3, 11, 12, 143; Post 40/4/2, Post 40/4/62; Post 42/36/124, Post 42/59/73, Post 42/61/205.

31. Post 10/24/156, Post 10/26/37.

32. The previous departure time had been between 2.30 am. and 4 pm. depending on the tide.

33. P.O.R. Post 10/24/88; Post 40/55/92G, Post 40/55/127G, Post 40/55/147G, Post 40/60/14K, Post 40/109/72C, Post 40/605/644; Post 42/70/96, Post 42/70/165, Post 42/70/205, Post 42/71/330, Post 42/98/433, Post 42/133/534.

34. P.O.R. 10A6, 10A11, 10A16; Post 9/132; Post 40/249/271, Post 40/619/206; Post 42/36/2, Post 42/109/280, Post 42/108/382, Post 42/109/587, Post 42/135/328.

35. P.O.R. Post 35/27/187; Post 40/105/84A, Post 40/100/33Y, Post 40/145/44, Post 40/235/186; Post 42/40/78, Post 42/97/247, Post 42/98/51, Post 42/103/272, Post 42/107/352.

36. Howard Robinson, *The British Post Office—A History* (Princeton pp. 230–1.

37. P.O.R. Post 30/474K (1814); Post 40/235/186; Post 42/107/352; *Second Report of the Select Committee on Postage* (1838), Appendix 45, p. 227; *1st-3rd reports of the Commissioners Appointed to Enquire Into the Management of the Post Office Department* (1835), pp. 25, 59: Alan Bates, *Directory of Mail Coach Services 1836* (Newton Abbot 1969), p. 60.

38. A bound volume of mail coach time bills is included in the Morton collection at Bruce Castle, Tottenham (546.4/21704); a further volume is in the Guildhall Library (Gr. 6.3.2.).

39. *The British Almanack and Companion* (1836), p. 75; *Second Report of the Select Committee on Postage* (1838), Appendix 45, p. 227; *1st-3rd Reports of the Commissioners Appointed to Enquire into the Management of the Post Office Department* (1835), pp. 25, 29; Charles G. Harper, *The Dover Road* (2nd edn. 1922), p. 3.

40. B.C. 546.4/21704; Guildhall Library, Gr. 6.3.2.; P.O.R. Post 40/605/644; Post 42/133/644: *Second Report of the Select Committee on Postage* (1838), Appendix 45, p. 227; *The British Almanack and Companion* (1836), p. 75; Herbert Joyce, *The History of the Post Office from its Establishment Down to 1836* (1893), p. 339.

41. B.C. 546.4/21704; Guildhall Library, Gr. 6.3.2.; P.O.R. Post 10/24/50; *The General Evening Post*, 5-7 Jan. 1786; *The London Chronicle*, No. 4555, 26-38 June 1786; *The Evening Mail*, No. 823, 4-6 June 1794; *Report from the Select Committee on Mail Coach Exemption* (1811), p. 47.

42. *1st-3rd Reports of Commissioners Appointed to Enquire into the Management of the Post Office Department* (1835), pp. 40, 59, 75, *7th Report* (1837), p. 54; *The British Almanack and Companion* (1836); Howard Robinson, *The British Post Office—A History* (Princeton 1948), p. 232.

43. The fall in rate in 1805 appears difficult to justify. The Rousseaux Price Index gives a figure of 175 for 1800 and 170 for 1805. After 1822 the index is for most years below 120 and the lower rate of 3d. is obviously justified.

44. P.O.R. Post 10/24/88; Post 40/109/72C, Post 40/191/29; Post 42/38/33, Post 42/104/446; *1st-3rd Reports of the Commissioners Appointed to Enquire into the Management of the Post Office Department* (1835), pp. 125f, *7th Report* (1837), p. 53; *Second Report of the Select Committee on postage* (1838), Appendix 45, p. 227; *Report from the Select Committee on Mail Coach Exemption* (1811), p. 47.

45. *The Mirror of the Times*, No. 514, 25 Jan.-1 Feb. 1806, No. 576 4-11 Apr. 1807.

46. H.L.R.O. Minutes of Evidence H.C., 1836, Vol. 36, South-Eastern Railway, 21 March p. 111.

47. *Report from the Select Committee on Mail Coach Exemption* (1811), p. 47; *First Report from the Select Committee on Postage* (1838), p. 331; Harper, *op. cit.*, p. 3; Thomas Burke, *Travel in England* (1842), p. 111.

48. P.O.R. Post 40/93/59T, Post 40/235/186, Post 40/664/573; Post 42/96/258, Post 42/107/352, Post 42/138/423.

49. P.O.R. Post 35/29/233; *Second Report of the Select Committee on Postage* (1838), p. 238.

50. P.O.R. Post 9/28, pp. 2, 3, 11, 12, 143; Post 40/499/36; Post 42/125/46;

51. P.O.R. Post 9/131; Post 40/61/81W, Post 40/65/63Y, Post 40/121/27L; Post 42/89/238, Post 42/90/56, Post 42/100/310.

52. Prices of oats in East Kent appear to have been appreciably higher than those of the United Kingdom as a whole, see graph p. 124.

53. P.O.R. Post 1/25/1; Post 40/92/95S, Post 40/161/97; Post 42/93/114, Post 42/103/144.

54. P.O.R. Post 40/126/27L, Post 40/235/186, Post 40/636/196; Post 42/98/51, Post 42/100/310, Post 42/107/352, Post 42/147/424.

55. P.R.O. Post 10/24/94, Post 10/26/72; Post 40/20/196A, Post 40/374/738; Post 42/66/75, Post 42/119/98; Brian Austen, 'Dover Post Office Packet Services', *Transport History*, Vol. 5, No. 1 (March 1972), pp. 42-3.

56. P.O.R. Post 40/11/199A, Post 40/449/749, Post 40/474/312; Post 42/39/97, Post 42/62/101, Post 42/121/300, Post 42/123/181; *Post Office Printed Notice No. 8*, May 1826.

57. P.O.R. Post 40/95/49V, Post 40/151/282, Post 40/275/65, Post 40/352/341, Post 40/361/539, Post 40/629/469; Post 42/96/414, Post 42/102/415, Post 42/110/352, Post 42/116/196, Post 42/115/86, Post 42/136/208.

58. *18th Report of the Commissioners of Inquiry into the Collection and Management of the Revenue Arising in Ireland and Great Britain* (1829), Appendix 31, p. 294; *Second Report of the Select Committee on Postage* (1838), Appendix 45, p. 227.

59. See p. 62.

60. *1st Report of the Select Committee on Postage* (1838), pp. 435, 444.

61. P.O.R. Post 40/13/196B, Post 40/14/56, Post 40/14/6C, Post 40/14/19C, Post 40/14/86C, Post 40/15/105C, Post 40/23/201B, Post 40/24/8C, Post 40/30/129F, Post 40/30/137F, Post 40/44/60 0, Post 40/105/101A, Post 40/190/280, Post 40/197/129F; Post 42/51/89, Post 42/51/111, Post 42/63/57, Post 42/63/74, Post 42/63/75, Post 42/63/92, Post 42/63/183, Post 42/63/200, Post 42/67/60, Post 42/67/127, Post 42/69/359, Post 42/69/375, Post 42/86/106, Post 42/98/85, Post 42/104/406, Post 42/104/417.

62. P.O.R. Post 40/65/63Y, Post 40/132/31M, Post 40/132/46; Post 42/90/56, Post 42/101/102, Post 42/101/450; Arthur Bryant, *The Years of Endurance* (1942), p. 285.

63. P.O.R. Post 40/9/50A, Post 40/9/65A, Post 40/28/119E; Post 42/40/76, Post 42/40/209, Post 42/61/158, Post 42/69/117.

64. P.O.R. Post 40/35/3X, Post 40/60/101V, Post 40/61/7W, Post 40/145/14; Post 42/71/65, Post 42/89/11, Post 42/89/97, Post 42/102/111.

65. P.O.R. Post 3/18, 3/19; Post 40/9/65A, Post 40/16/223C; Post 42/61/209, Post 42/64/80.

66. P.O.R. Post 35/46/203; Post 40/37/4K, Post 40/157/274, Post 40/158/292, Post 40/229/334; Post 42/71/330, Post 42/103/12, Post 42/103/27, Post 42/107/45.

67. P.O.R. Post 40/4/41, Post 40/307/547; Post 42/59/62, Post 42/113/107.

68. P.O.R. Post 3/12, 3/18, 3/19, 3/24, 3/25; Post 40/604/580; Post 42/133/420; *V.C.H. Kent*, Vol. 3 (1932), pp. 358f.

69. See Table 13, p. 93.

70. See pp. 94–7.

71. See pp. 97–9.

72. 24 Geo. III Sess. 2 cap. 25, 37 Geo. III cap. 18, 41 Geo. III cap. 7, 45 Geo III cap. 11, 52 Geo. III cap. 88.

73. See pp. 75, 79–80.

74. Schumpter-Gilboy Price Index for Consumer Goods, B. R. Mitchell and P. Deane, *Abstract of British Historical Statistics* (1962), pp. 468–9.

75. For information concerning the rise in the price of horse feed and subsequent rises in the cost of postal conveyance see pp. 79–80.

76. *Post Office London Directory* (20th edn. 1819), pp. 398–404.

77. *First Report of the Select Committee on Postage* (1838), pp. 17, 22; Henmeon, *op. cit.*, p. 246. For details of the methods used at this period to avoid postage, see Howard Robinson, *The British Post Office—A History* (Prrinceton 1948), pp. 282-6.

78. *First Report of the Select Committee on Postage* (1838), pp. 329-330. See also Table 12, p. 92. A rise in population between 1801 and 1841 of 131.8 per cent. should be compared with a rise of only 40 per cent. in postal revenue between 1800 and 1835.

79. P.O.R. Post 40/605/644; Post 42/133/534.

80. P.O.R. Post 40/30/101F, Post 40/30/102F, Post 40/48/68Q; Post 42/69/305, Post 42/69/307, Post 42/86/530.

81. P.O.R. Post 40/188/285; Post 42/104/409.

82. P.O.R. Post 40/72/90C; Post 42/92/329; Howard Robinson, *The British Post Office—A History* (Princeton 1948), pp. 147-8, 246-7, 283.

83. *H.C. Sessional Papers* 1814-5 (123) x 379; 1830 (548) xxv 361.

84. *Ibid.*, 1837-8 (87), xlv, 251. These were the only three Kentish offices able to provide figures.

85. *First Report of the Select Committee on Postage* (1838), Appendix 4, p. 444; *Second Report* (1838), Appendix E, No. 56, pp. 257, 259.

86. P.O.R. Post 42/93/598, Post 42/97/112; Howard Robinson, *The British Post Office—A History* (Princeton 1948), pp. 216-7.

87. P.O.R. Post 42/95/604, Post 42/96/421, Post 42/97/112.

88. P.O.R. Post 30, Pt. II/908X (1837); Post 35/31/147; Post 42/96/23.

89. 5 Geo. III cap. 25.

90. Howard Robinson, *The British Post Office—A History* (Princeton 1948), pp. 69-76, 207-218.

91. This Table includes Lamberhurst as a Kentish post town though the village is in fact situated on the county border. Routes originating from Kentish post towns but serving villages in Sussex have been included.

92. See Table of Kentish Penny posts on pp. 152-6.

93. P.O.R. Post 42/92/329, Post 42/95/616, Post 42/100/118, Post 42/103/531, Post 42/104/406, Post 42/104/409, Post 42/104/516, Post 42/108/50, Post 42/100/420, Post 42/111/82, Post 42/111/195, Post 42/132/315, Post 42/133/475.

94. P.O.R. Post 42/92/329, Post 42/100/118, Post 42/103/351, Post 42/104/402, Post 42/106/414, Post 42/108/50, Post 42/110/420, Post 42/113/62, Post 42/133/475, Post 42/138/266.

95. P.O.R. Post 35/29/203; Post 42/108/50, Post 42/118/732, Post 42/119/85, Post 42/132/315.

96. P.O.R. Post 40/284/401, Post 42/91/393; Post 42/111/82, Post 42/114/64, Post 42/114/133, Post 42/118/175, Post 42/118/238, Post 42/123/84, Post 42/123/212, Post 42/123/282.

97. P.O.R. Post 42/106/51, Post 42/110/120, Post 42/117/599, Post 42/133/475.

98. See Table 16, p. 96 and Table 20, pp. 108-10.

99. See Table 15, p. 96.

100. Henmeon, *op. cit.*, p. 246.

101. Excludes loss/profit on operation of the Wye-Ashford Penny Post which is now known.

102. P.O.R. Post 40/142/61S; Post 42/104/406, Post 42/101/619.

103. P.O.R. Post 40/606/644; Post 42/133/534; Howard Robinson, *The British Post Office—A History* (Princeton 1948), p. 218.

104. P.O.R. Post 40/139/51R, Post 40/191/29, Post 40/588/106; Post 42/101/469, Post 42/104/446, Post 42/132/215; Howard Robinson, *The British Post Office—A History* (Princeton (1948), pp. 193-4, map facing p. 198.

105. Howard Robinson, *THe British Post Office—A History* (Princeton 1948), pp. 132, 240.

106. P.O.R. Post 40/36/107I, Post 40/81/71K, Post 40/105/87A, Post 40/126/27L, Post 40/152/6, Post 40/275/65; Post 42/93/598, Post 42/98/55, Post 42/100/310, Post 42/100/441, Post 42/103/272, Post 42/110/352.

107. *Report from the Committee who were Appointed to Consider the Agreement Made with Mr. Palmer* (1797), p. 116.

108. P.O.R. Post 40/324/315; Post 42/114/298. F. E. Baines, *On the Track of the Mail Coach* (1895), p. 84 confuses this theft with that from the Dover coach in January 1827.

109. F. George Kay, *Royal Mail* (1951), p. 130f; P.O.R. Post 30/1044Z (1837).

110. *The Gentleman's Magazine,* August 1786; Charles G. Harper, *The Dover Road* (2nd edn. 1922), p. 217 records the date as 31 July 1789.

111. P.O.R. Post 40/53/135S, Post 40/56/132T, Post 40/73/99D, Post 40/77/105D; Post 42/87/468, Post 42/88/113, Post 42/92/106, Post 42/92/117; *The Evening Mail,* 2-4 July 1798, 21-24 Sept. 1798, 26-28 Sept. 1798; Baines, *op. cit.,* p. 84.

112. P.O.R. Post 40/20/125A, Post 40/20/139A, Post 40/35/26I, Post 40/77/28I, Post 40/35/37I, Post 40/35/39I, Post 40/35/45I, Post 40/35/53I, Post 40/35/69I, Post 40/70/23B, Post 40/151/285, Post 40/180/177, Post 40/630/687; Post 42/65/296, Post 42/65/313, Post 42/71/106, Post 42/71/109, Post 42/71/113, Post 42/71/124, Post 42/71/137, Post 42/71/148, Post 42/71/192, Post 42/91/84, Post 42/102/417, Post 42/104/95, Post 42/137/9.

113. P.O.R. Post 40/25/92C, Post 40/25/100C, Post 40/291/657, Post 40/471/211, Post 40/474/281; Post 42/68/70, Post 42/68/89, Post 42/111/515, Post 42/123/26, Post 42/123/132; Prosecution Briefs 1774-1836, Nos. 39, 46, 53, 58, 73, 107, 175, 190, 226, 255, 260, 285.

114. P.O.R. Post 10/6/126; Post 35/27/187; Post 40/301/314, Post 40/303/381, Post 40/623/402; Post 42/112/370, Post 42/112/457. Post 42/130/296.

115. P.O.R. Post 35/24/318, Post 35/24/325, Post 35/27/514, Post 35/29/197; Post 40/27/26E, Post 40/27/30E, Post 40/27/35E; Post 42/68/423, Post 42/68/428, Post 42/68/435; P.R.O. H033/1, 7 Dec. 1816; Baines, *op. cit.,* pp. 45-6.

116. P.O.R. Post 40/310/665; Post 42/113/286; *The Evening Mail,* 3-6 Aug. 1798.

117. P.O.R. Post 35/31/121; Post 40/226/271, Post 40/230/8, Post 40/239/275, Post 40/309/635; Post 42/106/594. Post 42/107/128, Post 42/107/368, Post 42/113/245.

118. See pp. 116–7.

119. P.O.R. Post 40/31/67G, Post 40/195/207, Post 40/195/218, Post 40/594/291, Post 40/600/455; Post 42/70/53, Post 42/104/608, Post 42/104/617, Post 42/132/519, Post 42/133/202. Edmund Vale, *The Mailcoach Men* (1960), p. 107.

Chapter 5

1. P.O.R. Post 40/35/37I, Post 40/48/63Q, Post 40/67/73Z, Post 40/78/10H, Post 40/137/80Q, Post 40/138/16R; Post 42/71/113, Post 42/86/526, Post 42/90/259, Post 42/93/89, Post 42/101/389, Post 42/101/424.

2. P.O.R. Post 40/139/38R; Post 42/101/456; B.C. 26IRAM/21723, 24 Nov. 1816.

3. P.O.R. Post 40/245/180, Post 40/246/192, Post 40/262/127; Post 42/36/107, Post 42/108/250, Post 42/108/272, Post 42/109/274; *H.C. Sessional Papers* 1836 (111), xlv, 373.

4. P.O.R. Post 3/24, 3/25; Post 40/70/15B, Post 40/70/28B, Post 40/75/75E; Post 42/91/70, Post 42/91/110, Post 42/92/298; Joyce, *op. cit.*, p. 334.

5. P.O.R. Post 40/193/111, Post 40/511/362, Post 40/638/289; Post 42/40/16, Post 42/104/516, Post 42/123/307, Post 42/138/7; *Second Report of the Select Committee on Postage* (1838), Appendix E, No. 40, p. 179.

6. P.O.R. Post 40/271/432, Post 40/430/307, Post 40/478/406, Post 40/489/756; Post 42/100/118, Post 42/120/204, Post 42/123/329, Post 42/124/245; James Phippen, *Colbran's New Guide for Tunbridge Wells* (Tunbridge Wells 1839), p. 400; J. Sprange, *The Tunbridge Wells Guide* (Tunbridge Wells 1786), p. 307.

7. P.O.R. Post 40/326/347; Post 42/114/340.

8. P.R.O. H042/211, 17 June 1795, H042/212, 23 June 1797, H042/213, 16 August 1798; *Report of the Committee of Secrecy Appointed to Enquire into the State of the Law in Respect of the Detaining and Opening of Letters at the General Post Office* (1844), pp. 10-11; G.P.O. *Printed Notice No. 19* (1816).

9. P.R.O. Post 35/43/315; P.R.O. H033/1, 29 Dec. 1820, 7 Jan. 1821, H033/3, 28 May 1832.

10. P.O.R. Post 40/20/125A, Post 40/20/139A, Post 40/39/77L, Post 40/44/5 0, Post 40/44/25 0, Post 40/44/44 0, Post 40/44/48 0, Post 40/45/115 0, Post 40/60/94V, Post 40/60/96V, Post 40/60/102V, Post 40/60/112V, Post 40/60/115V, Post 40/162/147; Post 42/65/296, Post 42/65/313, Post 42/72/77, Post 42/86/8, Post 42/86/45, Post 42/86/74, Post 42/86/81, Post 42/86/192, Post 42/88/621, Post 42/88/623, Post 42/88/14, Post 42/89/29, Post 42/89/36, Post 42/103/188; Prosecution Brief No. 53.

11. See Table 22, p. 127.

12. P.O.R. Post 40/550/680; Post 42/128/492.

13. P.O.R. Post 40/404/713; Post 40/589/275, Post 40/631/720; Post 42/119/47, Post 42/132/275, Post 42/137/66; *H.C. Sessional Papers* 1830 (293), 53.

14. P.O.R. Post 40/467/93, Post 40/503/154, Post 40/631/720, Post 40/646/657; Post 42/122/441, Post 42/125/234, Post 42/137/66, Post 42/139/49.

15. P.O.R. Post 35/26/60, Post 35/29/203, Post 35/31/86, Post 35/31/359; Post 40/642/484, Post 40/644/573, Post 40/646/537; Post 42/138/300, Post 42/138/423, Post 42/139/49.

16. P.O.R. Post 40/100/181, Post 40/156/204, Post 40/616/108, Post 40/618/146, Post 40/618/156, Post 40/618/163; Post 42/102/624, Post 42/105/98, Post 42/135/134, Post 42/135/209, Post 42/135/227, Post 42/135/241.

17. See Tables 23 and 24, pp. 128–131.

18. P.O.R. Post 40/644/573, Post 40/644/577; Post 42/138/423, Post 42/138/428; *Second Report of the Select Committee on Postage* (1838), Appendix E, No. 40, p. 179.

19. P.O.R. Post 40/193/111, Post 40/285/465, Post 40/588/20, Post 40/635/162; Post 42/104/516, Post 42/111/200, Post 42/129/237, Post 42/137/366.

20. P.O.R. Post 40/123/59I; Post 42/100/42; *Second Report of the Select Committee on Postage* (1838), Appendix E, No. 40, P. 179; Clifford, *op. cit.*, p. 172.

21. P.R.O. T22/28/418; *Second Report of the Select Committee on Postage* (1838), Appendix E, No. 40, p. 179.

22. P.O.R. Post 40/397/570; Post 42/118/601; *Second Report of the Select Committee on Postage* (1838), Appendix E, No. 40, p. 179; Howard Robinson, *The British Post Office—A History* (Princeton 1948), pp. 149–50.

23. P.O.R. Post 40/202/150.

24. P.O.R. Post 9/132/166; Post 40/80/5K, Post 40/198/335; Post 42/105/91.

25. P.O.R. Post 9/132/84, Post 9/132/101, Post 9/132/166, Post 9/132/263; Post 40/123/901; Post 42/100/97. Until July 1808 the post town was designated Tunbridge (i.e., Tonbridge), but the postmaster resided in and had his main office at Tunbridge Wells.

26. There appears to have been a degree of confusion in the Post Office itself over the differences between a sub-deputy and a receiver, e.g., the Post Office minute book records on 26 Oct. 1838 the appointment of a receiver at Rolvenden (P.O.R. Post 35/27/229), but the records of the Postmasters' Salary and Riding Book 1838–43, records the Rolvenden 'sub-deputy' (P.O.R. Post 9/132/166).

27. P.O.R. Post 9/132; Post 40/26/15D, Post 40/79/43I, Post 40/605/644; Post 42/68/250, Post 42/93/351, post 42/133/534.

Chapter 6

1. P.O.R. Post 10/27/50. J. R. Foxell and A. O. Spafford, *Monarchs of all they Surveyed—The Story of the Post Office Surveyors* (1952), p. 27.

2. P.O.R. Post 40/14/50A, Post 40/366/664, Post 40/590/167; Post 42/61/158, Post 42/117/160, Post 42/132/315.

3. P.O.R. Post 40/66/49Z, Post 40/137/80Q, Post 40/137/92Q, Post 40/138/10R, Post 40/138/16R; Post 42/90/226, Post 42/101/389, Post 42/101/405, Post 42/101/417, Post 42/101/424.

4. P.O.R. Post 40/31/9G, Post 40/193/123, Post 40/263/153, Post 40/384/243, Post 40/395/538, Post 40/404/715, Post 40/550/703; Post 42/69/392, Post 42/104/524, Post 42/109/310, Post 42/116/25, Post 42/118/537, Post 42/119/48, Post 42/128/517.

5. P.O.R. Post 40/88/12Q, Post 40/88/17Q, Post 40/87/78, Post 40/188/252; Post 42/95/183, Post 42/95/275, Post 42/95/284, Post 104/385.

6. *Second Report of the Select Committee on Postage* (1838), Appendix, p. 11, lists 320 petitions received 'this session of parliament in favour of Rowland Hill's scheme'. Only three of these were from Kent—one from the Maidstone Mechanics' Institute, and one each from individuals from Hythe and Goudhurst. No Kentish town council petitioned parliament, though in the nation at large 73 did so.

SELECT BIBLIOGRAPHY

(1) Manuscript Sources.

Post Office Records Office

Post 1 Treasury Letter Books (1686 onwards).

Post 3 Post Office Accounts (1685 onwards).

Post 9/131 Riding Work, 1791-2.

    9/145 Annual Salaries to Deputies, Bye and Cross Post, 1792.

    9/132 Postmasters' Salaries and Riding Work, 1838-43.

Post 10/5 Instructions to Mail Guards, 1790-1809.

    10/6 Instructions to Mail Guards, 1810-1841.

    10/7 Time Bills.

    10/8 and 9 Guarding the Horse Posts.

    10/24 and 25 Hasker's Report Books 1793-4.

    10/26 and 27 Hasker's Letter Books 1794-6.

Post 14/1 and 14/2 Bye and Cross Letter Office Reports 1757-1831.

Post 16/17 Ralph Allen's Instruction Book to Surveyors.

Post 35 Postmaster-Generals' Minute Books (1774 onwards).

Post 40 Postmaster-Generals' Reports from Surveyors (1791 onwards).

Post 42/35 to Post 42/52 Freeling's Minute Books.

Post 42/59 to Post 42/139 Postmaster-Generals' Report Books, 1792-1836.

Post 42/141 Observations by the Secretary and Postmaster-General on Letters received, 1803.

Post 94 Peover Papers (Papers of Col. Roger Whitley), 1672-77.

Post 96 Palmer Papers.

Post 97 Walsingham Papers.

Public Record Office

H033/1-3 Home Office Departmental (Post Office), 1784-1840.

H042/206-214 Home Office—Domestic, George III, 1782-99.

SP29 State Papers of the Reign of Charles II.

T22/17-28 Treasury—Out Letters, 1821-38.

Customs and Excise Record Offices

Customs 28/45 and 28/111. Minute Books, 1821 and 1835.
Customs 54 Dover Letter Books, 1817–1822.

Kent County Archives Office

Sandwich Borough Records Sa/C4 (1648 and 1662).

East Sussex County Record Office

Rye Corporation Records—Rye MS./50 (1786).
Sayer MS. 1450B.

British Library

G 6463—Proclamation of Henry Bishop, 1660.
Harleian MS. 7365 Thomas Gardiner's Survey of the Post
     Office.

House of Lords Record Office

Minutes of Evidence (HC), 1836, Vol. 36, South Eastern
     Railway Bill.

(2) **Printed Sources**

(a) Parliamentary.

*Report of the Committee . . . into Certain Abuses in the Post
     Office* (1787).
*10th Report of the Commissioners Appointed to Enquire into
     the Fees, Gratuities, Perquisites, etc.* (1788).
*Report from the Committee who were Appointed to Consider
     the Agreement made with Mr. Palmer* (1797).
Report from the Select Committee on Mail Coach Exemption
     (1811), 1810-11 (212), III, 707.
*18th Report of the Commission of Enquiry into the Collection
     of Revenue* (1829), 1829 (161), XI, 1.
22nd Report (1830), 1830 (647), XIV, 1.
*1st-3rd Reports of the Commissioners Appointed to Enquire
     into the Management of the Post Office Department*
     (1835), 1835 (313), XLVIII, 339, 1835 (542), XXVIII,
     487.

4th Report (1836), 1836 (49), XXVIII, 33.
6th Report (1836), 1836 (51), XXVIII, 145.
7th Report (1837), 1837 (70), XXXIV, Pt. I, 263.
1st Report from the Select Committee on Postage (1836),
     1837-8 (278), XX, Pt. I, 1.
2nd Report (1836), 1837-8 (658), XX, Pt. II, 1.
3rd Report (1838), 1837-8 (708), XX, Pt. I, 517.
Committee of Secrecy (1844), 1844 (582), XIV, 505.
Acts of Parliament, *Journal of the House of Commons* and
     House of Commons Sessional Papers as quoted.

(b) Other Printed Sources

Allen, Ralph, *Ralph Allen's Own Narrative,* ed. Adrian E.
     Hopkins (Bath 1959).
Andrews, J. H., 'Rye Harbour in the Reign of Charles II',
     Sussex Archaeological Collections, Vol. XCIV (Lewes
     1956).
Austen, Brian, 'Dover Post Office Packet Services 1633-1837',
     Transport History, Vol. 5, No. 1, March 1972.
Baines, F. E., *On the Track of the Mail Coach* (1895).
Blome, Richard, *Britannia* (1673).
British Almanack and Companion (1835, 1838, 1839).
Bryant, Arthur, *The Years of Endurance* 1793-1802 (1942).
Burke, Thomas, *Travel in England* (1942).
Calendar of Home Office Papers of the Reign of George III.
Calendar of State Papers Domestic (cited as *Cal. S.P. [Dom.]).*
Calendar of Treasury Books (cited as *Cal. T.B.).*
Calendar of Treasury Books and Papers (cited as *Cal. T.B. & P.).*
Cary's New and Correct English Atlas (1793).
Cary's New Itinerary (various edns. 1798-1828).
Cary's Traveller's Companion (1791).
Chalklin, C. W., *Seventeenth Century Kent* (1965).
Chamberlayne, E. and J., *The Present State of England* and
     The Present State of England and Ireland (various edns.
     1671-1726).
Clifford, J., *A Descriptive Guide of Tunbridge Wells* (n.d.);
     The Visitor's Guide to Tunbridge Wells and its Environs
     (1833).
Cobbett, William, *Rural Rides* (Penguin English Library) (1967).

Colbran, John, *Colban's New Guide for Tunbridge Wells,* ed. James Phippin (1839).

Court and City Kalender (1761 and 1765 edns.).

Deane, Phyllis and Cole, W. A., *British Economic Growth 1688-1959* (2nd edn. 1967).

Defoe, Daniel, *A Tour Through England and Wales.*

Dunlop, Sir, John, *The Pleasant Town of Sevenoaks* (Sevenoaks 1964).

Elliott, T. H., *State Papers Domestic Concerning the Post Office in the Reign of Charles II* (Bath 1964).

Ellis, Kenneth, *The British Post Office in the Eighteenth Century* (1958).

Evelyn, John, *The Diary of John Evelyn,* ed. E. S. de Beer (1959).

Evening Mail, 4/6 June, 7/9 June 1794, 23/26 Jan., 2/4 Feb. 1795, 2/4 July, 3/6 Aug., 21/24 Sept., 3/5 Oct. 1798.

Everitt, A. M., *The Community of Kent and the Great Rebellion 1640-60* (Leicester 1966).

Fiennes, Celia, *The Journeys of Celia Fiennes,* ed. Christopher Morris (1949).

Foxell, J. G. and Spafford, A. O., *Monarchs of all they Surveyed* (1952).

Fraser, Peter, *The Intelligence of the Secretaries of State and their Monopoly of Licensed News* (1956).

Gardiner, Thomas, *A General Survey of the Post Office 1677-1682,* ed. Foster W. Bond (Bath 1958).

Gent, G. F., *The Secretary's Guide* (1759).

Gentleman's Magazine.

Harper, C. G., *The Dover Road* (2nd edn. 1922). *Stage Coach and Mail in Days of Yore* (1903).

Harris, S., *The Coaching Age* (1885).

Henmeon, J. C., *The History of the British Post Office* (Harvard 1912).

Historic Manuscript Commission Reports (cited as *H.M.C.*).

Hyde, J. W., *The Early History of the Post in Grant and Farm* (1894).

Joyce, Herbert, *The History of the Post Office from its Establishment down to 1836* (1893).

Kaye, F. George, *The Royal Mail* (1951).

Kentish Gazette, 1790-1816.

London Carriers' Directory (1793).

London Chronicle or Universal Evening Post, Nos. 980, 4555.

London Courant, Noon Gazette and Daily Advertiser, 17 Feb. 1782.

London Gazette, Nos. 2086, 8406, 8433, 8442, 8443, 9592.

Maudslay, A., *Highways and Horses* (1888).

Mercurius Politicus 13/20 Aug. 1657.

Mitchell, B. R. and Deane, Phyllis, *Abstract of English Historical Statistics* (1962).

Mogg, Edward, *Patterson's Roads* (various editions).

Ogilby, John, *Britannia* (1675).

Oulton, W. C., *The Traveller's Guide* (1805).

Owen's New Book of Roads (2nd edn. 1799).

Parkes, Joan, *Travel in England in the Seventeenth Century* (1925).

Piggot & Co.'s New Commercial Directory (various editions).

Plan for the Better Regulation of the Footscray Post (1768).

Playford, John, *Vade Mecum, or the Necessary Companion* (1679).

Post Office Annual Directory (various editions).

Post Office London Directory (various editions).

Presnail, James, *Chatham—The Story of a Dockyard Town* (Chatham 1952).

Robertson, Alan, *Post Roads, Post Towns, Postal Rates 1635–1840* (Pinner 1961).

Robinson, Howard, *Britain's Post Office* (1953); *The British Post Office—A History* (Princeton 1948); *Carrying British Mails Overseas* (1964).

Royal Kalender (1784 edn.).

St. James's Chronicle or British Evening Post, Nos. 983, 1478, 1663, 1665, 1683, 1688.

St. James's Evening Post, 2/3 May 1747.

Smith's New Map of England and Wales (1821).

Sprange, J., *The Tunbridge Wells Guide* (1786).

Staff, Frank, *The Penny Post* (1964).

Stitt-Dibden, W. G. (ed.), *The Post Office 1635–1720* (Bath 1960).

Stowe, John, *Survey of London,* ed. Strype (1720).

Taylor, John, *The Carriers' Cosmographie* (1637).

The Times, 3 Oct. 1798.

Town and County Magazine.
Tristram, W. Outram, *Coaching Days and Coaching Ways* (2nd edn. 1893).
Vale, Edmund, *The Mail Coach Men* (1960).
Victoria County History—Kent, Vol. 3 (1932) (cited as *V.C.H.*).
Whitehall Evening Post or London Intelligencer, No. 379. 14/16 July 1748.

100 Guineas
REWARD.

GENERAL POST-OFFICE, 21st June, 1826.

Whereas in the Night of Tuesday the 6th Instant,

Seven Mail Bags
AND A
BOX OF LETTERS,

were feloniously Stolen from the Dover Mail, between Chatham
and Rainham, in the County of Kent.

Whoever will come forward and give such Information as
may lead to the apprehension and conviction of the Offender or
Offenders shall receive a Reward of

ONE HUNDRED GUINEAS.

The Bags and Box were found on the following Morning in a Field, within
a short distance of the Star Public House, Chatham Hill; near which spot
the Robbery is supposed to have been committed.

If any Person concerned in the said Robbery, or knowing thereof, will
surrender himself, and make discovery, whereby the other Person or Persons who committed the same may be apprehended and brought to Justice,
such discoveror will be entitled to the said Reward, and will also receive His
Majesty's most gracious Pardon.

By Command of the Postmaster-General,

F. FREELING, Sec'.

Harmsll, Printer, Wine-Office-Court, Fleet-Street

(By courtesy of the Post Office)

LOST,

The following Dover Bank Notes,

Which were fent by Poft from DOVER, the 6th inftant, directed to *Mr. F. Finmore, Mafter of the Lord Nelfon Cutter,* *SHEERNESS:* the Letter has not been delivered.

It is therefore requefted if the Notes are offered in payment, that immediate notice may be given to *Mr. Finmore,* or to *Mr. Bryan Bentham, Sheernefs*; or to *Meffrs. Fector, and Minet, DOVER.*

No.				No.			
6281,	—19 July,	1798,	30*l.*	*a* 2879,—	1 Nov.	1799,	10*l.*
3248,	—13 October,	1797,	25*l.*	*a* 2862,—	1 Nov.	1799,	10*l.*
1722,	— 7 July,	1797,	15*l.*	6778,—	25 July,	1798,	5*l.*
955,	—12 May,	1797,	10*l.*	9823,—	24 Nov.	1798,	5*l.*
1501,	—20 May,	1797,	10*l.*	*a* 1312,—	17 April,	1799,	5*l.*
2363,	—17 Auguft,	1797,	20*l.*	*a* 2178,—	21 Oct.	1799,	5*l.*

February 10, 1800.

Townfon, Printer, Chatham.

(By courtesy of the Post Office)

June 1 18*27*

Mrs   *Ruddick, Wid.*

HIS Majesty's Postmaster General
having been pleased to accept of the Recommendation of
Sir William Curtis Bt.
to appoint you their Deputy at *Ramsgate*
in the Room of *your Husband, deceased*
I am to desire you will send me the Names, Professions, and
Places of Abode of Two sufficient Persons, to be bound with you
in the Sum of *One thousand Pounds* —
for the due and faithful Discharge of your Duty, that a Bond
may be made out and sent for you and them to execute, and a
Deputation granted you.

You will state whether you or the Sureties you propose have
entered into any Engagements of a similar Nature to any other
Departments of the Revenue, and if so, their Nature and Extent.

Inclosed are some Forms of the Oath of Office which is
directed by the Act of 9th Queen Ann, to be taken by all Persons
who are to be employed in sorting or delivering of Letters, to
qualify them for the Employment.

I am,

Your obedient Servant,

[signature]

Secretary

J Hartnell. Printer, Wine-office-court, Fleet-street,
for His Majesty's Stationery Office.

GENERAL POST OFFICE,

21st JANUARY, 1824.

FIFTY POUNDS
Reward.

WHEREAS on the Evening of Tuesday the 20th Instant, several Mail Bags of Letters were feloniously stolen from the Mail Cart between Rye and Northiam.

Whoever shall apprehend the Person or Persons who committed the said Felony, will be entitled to the above Reward; Twenty Pounds upon commitment of the Offender or Offenders for Trial, and the remaining Thirty Pounds upon Conviction.

The following are the Mail Bags stolen:

Rye and London, *100*
Rye and Lamberhurst, *200*
Rye and Tunbridge, *100*
Rye and Seven Oaks, *100*
Rye and Bromley. *100*

By Command of the Postmaster-General,

FRANCIS FREELING,

Secretary.

Printed by J. Hartnell, Wine-Office-Court, Fleet Street, for His Majesty's Stationery Office.

(By courtesy of the Post Office)

INDEX